BEGINNING RASPBERRY PI 2

CHARLES DANIELS

Suntime Publishing

2015

Dedication

This book is dedicated to anyone that wishes to learn and share their knowledge. A special thanks to the following individuals that provided their skills, knowledge and time to make this book possible. By sharing our knowledge we will make this world a better place for everyone.

A special thanks to Jim Butler, Trevor Stevens, Neal Roper, Lorne Orson, Alison Watson, Sandra Miller, Cynic, Suntime Box community, and Natalie Masters for all your input, advice and time. A special thank you to Kohina, Rob Hubbard, Martin Walker, Martin Galway, and the Raspberry Pi community.

About this book

This book will give you an understanding of the Raspberry Pi 2 and how it can best be used in the world today. It will take a look at the Raspberry Pi 2 in detail and will explain how to use the operating systems available. You will learn the various programs that can be used with it and will explore how to configure them. You will learn the command line interface (CLI) and how it can be used when the Raspberry Pi desktop isn't available.

You will gain technical knowledge of how databases and web servers function and you will understand the use of WordPress which is used by professional web designers. Finally you will take a look at the Python programming language which will give you the technical ability to write your own programs and even start contributing to the Raspberry Pi community.

What will you get form this book?

Beginning Raspberry Pi 2 will teach you how to use, program and understand the Raspberry Pi 2. It will help you by using practical examples, visual images and diagrams to explain many of the concepts used for learning the Raspberry Pi and programming in general.

You will learn about the hardware and software that makes up the Raspberry Pi and as a bonus you will be learning Linux without any additional effort and to some extent the Unix operating system, which is the bigger brother of GNU/Linux. Most Raspberry Pi operating systems are based on a type of Linux operating system. The commands and functionality that you will learn for this book will also apply GNU/Linux. You will learn how real world servers are set-up and maintained including the Apache web server, and mySql database. You will also gain a basic understanding of system administration which again can be applied to Linux in the real world.

Do I need any previous or programming experience?

No. All the concepts in this book will build upon the previous chapters and you will gain knowledge from the ground up.

How has this book been designed?

This book has been designed as though you are following a course. It is sectioned into multiple chapters that contain smaller but more focused topics. These topics contain information on a particular subject so that each topic will teach you the foundation for the next topic. Each chapter will build upon the previous one which in turn will build up your knowledge as you progress.

For example, the first couple of chapters will guide you through understanding basic computer science concepts followed by what makes up the Raspberry Pi. This will give you a brief overview of some of the operating systems available for the Raspberry Pi and will help you understand how to connect it all together. Further into the chapter you will learn how to login to the Raspberry Pi and learn the basics of how it functions. When this foundation is in place you will move onto more advanced topics.

CONTENTS

Chapter 1 Raspberry Pi 2 3

Chapter 2 The Internet of Things (IoT)...............................13

Chapter 3 Creating the Operating System 33

Chapter 4 Setting up the Raspberry Pi 2 41

Chapter 5 Using the raspberry pi 51

Chapter 6 The Command Line Interface (CLI)...................68

Chapter 7 Wi-Fi and Networking 88

Chapter 8 System Maintenance...106

Chapter 9 Web Servers & Databases 120

Chapter 10 Installing & Using WordPress 140

Chapter 11 Programming Concepts 153

Chapter 12 The Python Programming Language 166

Beginning Raspberry Pi 2

Chapter 1
Raspberry Pi 2

The Raspberry Pi 2 is a low cost computer that has the ability to compete with some PC's that are available on the market today. The Raspberry Pi 2 can browse the internet, create word processing documents, spreadsheets, create web sites, play movies, play games, work in the cloud and it can even be used to create music. Probably the most amazing thing is that the Raspberry Pi can interact with the outside world allowing it to be connected to robots, cameras, musical instruments, sensors, printers and more. The only limitation is your imagination which is infinite, so you can imagine the possibilities. So where did it all begin?

The Raspberry Pi started out its life with the idea of reliving the philosophy of the older days of 8 bit computing. This philosophy captured the idea of having fun while learning. During the 1980's a range of 8 bit computers emerged including the Commodore 64, Spectrum 48K, Acorn, Amstrad CPC and Dragon 32. These computers were extremely fun and many programmers, musicians, graphic artists owe their careers to these great but limited machines. People would exchange ideas, swap programming techniques and learn as much as they could. Demo scene swapping parties appeared in which programmers, artist and musicians would demonstrate their skills and exchange ideas. The origin of gaming parties also started here and the first gaming communities were born. This was the dawn of the home computer and a new world began to emerge with a generation of new skills. The younger generation of that day learned without realising they were learning. They learned by exploring, experimenting and having fun. Knowledge and ideas were gained simply by experimenting as one community.

As time progressed and 8 bit became 16 bit, 16 bit became 32 bit etc, the older 8 bit machines made their way into people's attics and were simply forgot. Computing and fun became almost separate entities over time as computers just seemed to exist for business use and became a tool.

The Raspberry Pi foundation wanted to put the idea of learning while having fun back into computing. Eben Upton, one of the trustees of the Raspberry Pi Foundation realised that this had been lost in the generation of children. It was realised that children leaving school really didn't understand the basics of how computers actually functioned and became simply a user of computers. He decided to get a group of teachers, enthusiasts and academics together to create a device that would not only teach children computing but would also inspire them. The Raspberry Pi was born.

The Raspberry Pi has seen many iterations since its

inception in 2011 but it wasn't until early 2012 that it was official released. It has been developed in Cambridge by the Raspberry Pi Foundation and is manufactured at the Sony facility in Wales, UK with a minority of devices being made in China. Since then the Raspberry Pi community have seen many additions, versions and models. Model A first appeared with limited memory and only 2 USB ports but Model A+, B and B+ improved on these limitations and with it came the ability to create better and more imaginative projects.

Today we have the Raspberry Pi 2 model B that is both powerful and up to 6 times faster than its previous versions. It is still only a fraction of the cost of a PC. It is a very small computer and is only slightly larger than the size of a credit card. The Raspberry Pi has opened the doors to children and adults around the world that could not afford the higher price tags of traditional computers and laptops. This has enabled beginners, enthusiasts and experts to learn, create and program computers without the associated cost of learning.

The new Raspberry Pi 2 offers an outstanding quad-core chip with double the memory of the previous Raspberry Pi bringing it up to 1G of RAM. The Raspberry Pi can now be seen as a fully working PC at an extremely low price tag. Backwards compatibility is guaranteed so any previous programs that have been written for the Pi will still work.

The Raspberry Pi 2 contains an ARM processor which are used in small devices including mobile phones, hand held mobile gaming devices and other small digital devices. ARM processors are extremely efficient, power resourceful and remarkably fast. The ARM processor fits perfectly well with the Raspberry Pi which has the capability to interface with the outside world and is extremely fast. Some of the devices include printers, lights, LEDS, TV's, robots and more.

There are some differences between a traditionally PC and the Raspberry Pi 2 but not many. For example the Raspberry Pi 2 does not have a hard drive to store data but relies on the micro SD card for the booting up and storing of its information. The micro SD card contains the operating system and programs which will allow the user to perform various functions.

The operating system gives instructions to the Raspberry Pi based on system services such as maintenance operations. These include checking the micro SD card for errors, releasing unused resources and managing user input. It manages the whole system including its programs, user interactions and the general running of the system. You can think of the operating system as the interface between you and the hardware. You will request an action and the operating system will perform the task. For example you could issue the delete command to delete a file. This command is passed to the operating system which will perform the delete action.

The software that is available for the Raspberry Pi 2 and previous models use the open source philosophy. Open source refers to something that can be freely modified, viewed and distributed because it's design is publically accessible. This means that it is free of restrictions and is in most cases free of cost. Other companies like Apple and Microsoft charge for the use of their software but the Raspberry Pi uses the open source concept and therefore it keeps the cost to an absolute minimum. Although at the time of writing Microsoft have announced that Windows 10 will be freely available for the Raspberry Pi 2. In most cases the cost for software is absolutely free because many people from around the world have contributed to the software for free. If programmers have access to the programs code which is referred to as *Source Code* then other programmers can examine, improve and fix any problems with the program. This is the fundamental element of Open Source.

What has been done with the Raspberry Pi so far? Enthusiasts and businesses from all across the globe have created amazing projects from small arcade machines to taking pictures from space. Some projects that are available is a garage door opener. This project allowed a user to use Siri on an Apple iPhone that communicates with the Raspberry Pi and opens an electric garage door. Raspberry Pi in The Sky project allowed a Raspberry Pi to be attached to a camera which was placed inside a hot air balloon. The hot air balloon took pictures of the Earth below. A retro emulator gaming console was created that allows a user to relive their old gaming days by installing thousands of old retro computers games. The Raspberry Pi laptop project is a self contained laptop complete with screen. A Remote Controlled Robot that uses the Python programming language to issue commands to the robot. A wearable Pi. This project was similar to the Google Glass project which allowed a user to wear glasses and interact with their Raspberry Pi. These are just some of the projects available but there is so much more that can be done. You should now start seeing how powerful the Raspberry Pi can be and the Raspberry Pi 2 just became even more powerful.

Take a look at the image below for an overview of what the Raspberry Pi 2 consists of.

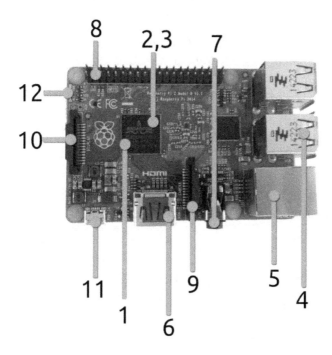

The main components are

1. The 900MHz next generation Quad Core ARM Cortext-A7 CPU which can process and perform calculations on data at lightning speed. The processor can deliver up to 6 times the performance of the model B+.

2. 1GB of RAM. One thing to note here is that this 1GB of RAM is shared with the GPU memory. This means you can allocate a majority of this memory to graphics processing if you are using your display output for 3D graphics etc.

3. GPU (Graphics Processing Unit) Broadcom Video Core IV 3D graphics core. This is used to process multimedia, 3D and graphic calculations which allows the Raspberry Pi to display smooth graphics.

4. 4x USB 2.0 ports. These are used for plugging in your keyboard, mouse, Wi-Fi, Bluetooth adapter or hard drive for external storage.

5. 1x Ethernet port 10/100Mpbs for plugging into a wired network.

6. HDMI output for video display. You can plug this into a TV or monitor that has a HDMI port.

7. 3.5mm audio and video output jack.

8. 40 GPIO pins. These pins can be used to connect to devices outside of the Raspberry Pi including robots, sensors etc.

9. Camera interface (CSI) which uses a 15 pin MIPI connector for connecting a camera.

10. Display interface (DSI) port connecting a touch screen display.

11. Micro USB Power source. You can plug in your power adapter to power up the Raspberry Pi 2.

12. LED lights for power and SD card access.

Compatibility

The existing software for the Raspberry Pi is still compatible with the Raspberry Pi 2 and any Python programs that you have written will still work. The original Pi used the ARMv6 processor chip but the latest model users the Cortext-A7 architecture. This means that the Raspberry Pi 2 can now run a wide range of operating systems including Android and Windows 10. This is a huge step forward as this will open the Raspberry Pi to an even wider community.

The Raspberry Pi 2 uses a micro SD card which means you are unable to just plug in your existing SD card which is physically larger. The GPIO pins are 100% compatible with the previous Model B+ which means that any interfacing with the outside world will still work.

Summary

You now have a brief understanding of why the Raspberry Pi emerged and why we have the latest model today. You also know what the Raspberry Pi is capable of and you are aware of the existing and ongoing projects that the community have accomplished with it. You also learned about the various components that make up the Raspberry Pi and what each component is used for.

CHAPTER 2
THE INTERNET OF THINGS (IOT)

To begin with you will need to have some basic understanding of the terminology used in the field of computer science and computers. Why is this required if you are learning about the Raspberry Pi? For those starting out in computers it is a good idea to get a feel for the terminology and how the rest of the world is using it. Part of the learning process is to understand how computers fit into our environment and how the Raspberry Pi is part of this. The Raspberry Pi also has its roots based on the ideas and technologies of the Internet of Things.

You do not need any previous knowledge of computers or programming as this chapter is designed to give you an insight into what to expect and the rest you will learn as we go along. If you are comfortable with the concepts of hardware, software, web servers, the internet of things and how computers and networks work in general then you can jump to the next chapter which describes the Raspberry Pi 2.

The concept of the Internet of Things dates back to 1982 when a modified soda machine was connected to a network that sent data to a remote device. Today the Internet has advanced so much that these devices can now connect on mass to the internet due to the advancement of IPv6, the reduction in size of embedded devices and cost reduction. We are now on the cusp of this emerging technology and you are perfectly placed to witness this technology explosion.

What is The Internet of Things?

The internet of things describes the connectivity of embedded devices. These devices range from washing machines, mobiles phones, computers, home automation systems, alarms, cars, traffic lights and even connected cities and power grids. These devices are sometimes called Smart Objects because they are aware of the internet and other connected devices around them. This interconnection will bring in a new era which also brings with it the term called *Big Data*. This means that each of these devices will produce a vast amount of data which will increase the traffic on the internet immensely. Some of this data will need to be stored so it can be analysed and acted upon. Some of this data will be used by other embedded devices for their input for their next action.

Currently some TV's have this ability already built in. Smart TV's for example have the capability to go online and stream movies and apps directly to the TV. They can even update themselves to include additional functions. The Internet of Things will be able to cover a range of areas including healthcare, manufacturing, environmental monitoring, space activity monitoring, media, energy management, transport and other small and large scale frameworks.

What is Computer Science?

Computer Science is the study, discipline and understanding of computers using a scientific approach. This includes the design, concept, programming, engineering, applications, mathematical and scientific principles underlying every kind of computing system. Some fields in Computer Science focus on implementing computation for subjects as encryption, computer security or astronomy. Other fields of study such as artificial intelligence (A.I) can take on an immense area of study consisting of computation and research which involves problem-solving, decision making and communication. Some of which attempts to duplicate behaviour in humans and animals using artificial intelligence.

Computer Science covers a broad range of industries and subjects which continue to emerge each day. Constant research, design and time is dedicated to the development of mobile phones, networks, communications, hardware, software, health, space exploration and many far reaching fields of study.

The computer

Most people are so accustomed to using computers on a daily basis but are not really aware of the underlying functionality that makes them function. This is because the large manufacturers of computers and software try and make using computers simple by hiding the complexity of it all. This is done in a number of ways by using graphic interfaces, icons, touch screens and speech recognition to interact with the computer. In order to use a computer you do not need an understanding of the technology and functionality in order to put it to use. A mobile/cell phone for example will allow you to make a call without you understanding how the call is placed. To some extent you may not care, you are only interested in speaking to the other person on the end of the phone.

How do we define a computer?

A computer is an electronic device that has the ability to manipulate data. Manipulation of data can include storage, retrieval and the processing of data. Inside a computer you will find a motherboard, a central processing unit also known as a CPU, memory and some type of storage device such as a hard drive or in the case of the Raspberry Pi 2 it is a micro SD card. Computers will also have some type of input device such as a keyboard or a mouse and a way of displaying its output. A monitor is an example of a device that receives input and displays the results on screen. In the case of the Raspberry Pi a TV or a monitor can be used for its output device.

Hardware

When we speak of hardware we are referring to something physical that can be held. Hardware is any part of the computer or device that is physical. Examples of hardware are computer memory, hard drives and SD cards because they are physical objects. Keyboards and mobile devices are examples of hardware but a web page displaying some text and an image isn't.

Software

Software is a collection of instructions or programs which tell the computer what to do. Software cannot be touched and only exists inside the computer's memory. Some examples of software are web browsers, a computer game or a word processor. Software needs some type of hardware to run on and just as your brain requires a body to perform actions, software needs hardware. You will often hear the term software and applications used in the same context but there is a difference.

Application Software

Application software is computer software that is designed to perform various tasks to help the user in their day to day activity. This could be a business that needs to print T-shirts. They would need some type of graphics program such as Photoshop CS6. Photoshop does not come as standard with any computer and therefore it is an application.

Applications are software programs that come in many forms. This is often sub divided and labelled as utility programs, integrated, bespoke or custom, generic and specific. Applications are written to perform a specific task or tasks. A word processor is an application because its function is to perform only that task.

A utility program can be a backup program or a program that maintains the health of your Raspberry Pi software. This type of software is a generic application that has not been written for any type of business but is general to all businesses.

Specific software on the other hand has only one purpose. Sage accounts or quick books accountancy software is a good example because only businesses would use this software. A home user would probably not need to use this.

Integrated software is defined as a collection of software with a common set of commands. Microsoft Office suite is an example because it contains everything that a day to day business or educational institute may need.

A bespoke application on the other hand has been written for a specific purpose when there isn't any software to perform the task. For example, Google maps may want to update their maps using live streaming technology instead of using out of date photographs. This software will have to written from the ground up in order to achieve this. Bespoke applications can be expensive because it will be time consuming writing applications from scratch.

GUI (Graphical User Interface)

A GUI is a graphical interface that allows the interaction between the user and the operating system. This makes using a computer easier. Before the days of graphic interfaces users would have to learn complicated commands that would be entered using a terminal. The commands would be complicated and often very long and prone to typos. GUI's can enhance the user experience by providing nice visual graphics and an intuitive way of using programs without the need to remember commands. This makes using a graphical interface more productive. The Raspberry Pi desktop is an example of a graphical user interface.

Memory

The Raspberry Pi uses two main types of memory as do computers in general. These are RAM and ROM.

RAM

RAM is very fast but is volatile meaning that it must have continuous power in order to store the data. If there is a power interruption the memory will be cleared and the data will be lost. This temporary memory is used by applications, the GUI and the operating system.

ROM

ROM is memory that cannot be changed by any application or program including the operating system. The memory stored in ROM will always be there even after the hardware has been powered off.

EPROM

This type of memory is declared as an Erasable

Programmable Read Only Memory. It is a type of chip that has the ability to remember data when the power supply has been switched off but can be erased using an ultra violet light and then reprogrammed.

Storage

Computers can store information permanently in various ways. Currently the most common way of storing data is to the cloud, a hard drive or in the case of the Raspberry Pi the SD card. Other types of devices can also be used include DVD's, USB flash drives, removable hard drives and Blu-ray discs.

Storage capacity is measured in numerous forms depending on the size of the storage device. The smallest representation of storage is a bit. Following this and increasing in size are bytes, kilobyte, megabyte, gigabyte, terabyte and petabyte. Higher capacity storage exists after these but at the time of writing terabytes are commonly used in laptops and PC's.

Many millions of bits are used to store data in memory and this can be thought of as millions of LED lights all aligned in rows one after the other.

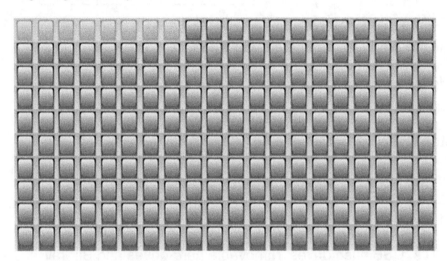

All of these millions of bits are grouped together to represent data. As an example imagine that 8 Bits represents a series of 8 lights. Each of these lights are currently off as indicated by a zero so nothing is lit up. If a light is switched on, this would indicate that this bit turned on.

The diagram above displays the first 8 bits of memory with some data stored in that location, be it a very simplified representation. You can think of the lights that are now lit up as a sequence of 1's. When the light is off it is 0.

It is often easier to group these bits so we can visually see them better.

[8 BITS]
00000000

If you wanted to represent two 8 bits or 16 bits in total then it would look like this.

```
[     16 BITS     ]
00000000 00000000
```

Now we will represent 32 bits.

```
[               32 BITS             ]
00000000 00000000 00000000 00000000
```

You can see in the diagram below how all bits are represented.

```
[ 8 BITS ][ 8 BITS ][ 8 BITS ][ 8 BITS ]
[     16 BITS     ][     16 BITS     ]
[               32 BITS             ]
00000000 00000000 00000000 00000000
```

The problem here is that the number becomes increasing larger to read and write out each time. Therefore users of computers will tend to represent the numbers in another way by grouping the numbers into easily manageable terms. A byte for example is simply a group of 8 bits, 2 bytes would be 16 bits.

8 bits   = 1 byte

00000000   = 1 byte

The chart below displays a list of measurements of data storage starting with the smallest to the largest.

Size	Is equal to
8 bits	= 1 byte
1024 bytes	= 1 kilobyte
1024 kilobytes	= 1 megabyte
1024 megabytes	= 1 gigabyte
1024 gigabytes	= 1 terabyte

Programs and people will try and represent their data in its simplest form.

Megahertz (MHz)

Megahertz is often used to measure the processing speed of memory in millions per second. An example might be that the Intel Compute Stick has a 800Mhz processor which means that it can possibly process data 800 million times per second.

What is information?

Take a look at the following two sentences which are about making a pizza.

Place 1 jar of pizza sauce over 1 pizza base. Spread 100g of cheese on top of the pizza sauce. Slice 2 peppers and 200g of ham and spread over the pizza.

The above information makes perfect sense because it contains all the information we need to create a pizza. When instructions contain everything that we need to understand the data, this is called information. Now the question arises, "What is data?"

What is data?

Read the following.

- 1 jar of pizza sauce
- 1 pizza base
- 100g of cheese
- 2 peppers
- 200g of ham

This explains what is required to make a pizza but not how to create a pizza. This is called data. Data comes in many forms including sequences of numbers, names, food or a mixture of sequences.

Take a shopping list for example.

- 2 Apples
- 1 Can of oil
- 1 Tin of paint
- 1 Raspberry Pi
- 200g of ham

This shopping list above contains a mixture of data from food items to paint. It does not explain how we are using these items. Sometimes data is represented visually to make it easier to understand. Some examples are pie charts, scatter plots, graphs and heat maps.

The following is considered information

- Get me 5 eggs please.
- I ran 5 miles this morning.

However, 5 eggs or 5 miles isn't considered information because it is just data and doesn't explain how or what to do with 5 eggs or miles.

The Internet

You are already familiar with the internet and its possibilities but you need to understand what really makes up the internet. Billions of computers and devices are located on and around the globe each connected to each other via the internet. Mobile phones, computers, fridge freezers, satellites and cars to name a few can communicate with each other using the internet. A computer in China can communicate with a home appliance in Italy. These devices communicate using the internet to send data back and forth.

If you were to map out the internet it would look like a huge connected spider web over the earth.

Web sites are located around the earth and are stored on web servers. Web servers are very fast computers that have the purpose of delivering information in the form of web pages to a user. If you visit http://www.suntimebox.com using your web browser then a web page will be returned to you. This web server is currently located in the Netherlands and the sole purpose of this web site is to display web pages.

Programs

A program is a set of instructions written in a programming language that the computer will execute to perform a task. For example the task of a web browser is to display web pages.

A program might read like this.

Get a cup.
Add a tea bag.
Boil the kettle.
When the kettle is boiled pour into a cup.
Add milk.
Add sugar.
Stir with a spoon.
Remove tea bag.

This program is translated by the computer into a program which is made up of zero and ones. The job of the CPU is to translate the binary instructions so that it can perform the actions. Below is a short sample of a program in binary.

0101 1111 1010 1011 1111 1010 0110 1110

Programming Languages

Programming languages are used to create a program for a specific task. Many programming languages exists and while some focus on a specific area of computing and mathematics others are more generalised. Later chapters will define the specifics of the languages available for the Raspberry Pi.

Operating Systems

In order to run programs there has to be a master program which manages all other programs. This type of program is called an operating system and every computer requires one in order for it to do anything useful. The operating system also manages time sharing between the programs and manages the computer's hardware. The operating system will act as a go between for the programs running and the computer hardware. Examples of operating systems are Microsoft's Window 10, Apples iOS, GNU/Linux, Debian Linux, Android OS and Chrome OS.

Networks

Computer networks are made up of a group of computers, servers or devices. A client, which can be a computer, phone or a Raspberry Pi will request information from a server and the server returns this information to the client. When you are visiting a web site your web browser is the client and the web site it is contacting is the server.

When a client asks the server for this information it is called a **client request**.

www.amazon.co.uk

Ports

Servers listen out for client requests using ports. A port is like a door on a computer. The client will knock on the door and ask the server for some information. If the computer has some data it wants to give to the client it will send the data back. Each port has a number. Some of these numbers are reserved so that when a client sends a request for information, it always knocks on the correct door. By default, web browsers will request their web pages using port 80 but some web sites are required to use a secure connection. Banking, financial and any web sites that are accepting credit card payments are required to use something called a Secure Socket Layer or SSL for short. This encrypts or scrambles the information so that anyone examining it will be unable to read the data. A secure socket layer will use port 443 and most web browsers will display a padlock when the connection is secure.

Summary

You now have a basic understanding of what the Internet of Things and computer science is. You are aware of the areas of research it can be used in and how the ongoing development is being used in the world today. You also have some background knowledge on what makes up a computer and its memory and storage capabilities. Bits have been described and how they are represented inside the computer.

You have a understanding of the bits, bytes etc and how they are grouped to simplify their representations when reading them. We also touched upon programming languages, networks, the internet and how clients and servers communicate. Operating systems have also been explained in simple terms and why they are needed.

Don't be discouraged if the above seems like it is too much to take in. Over time you will gain further understanding of computers and computer science and how information and technology fit together in today's world.

CHAPTER 3
CREATING THE OPERATING SYSTEM

The Raspberry Pi has many different operating systems to choose from. Each operating system has been designed for either specific requirements such as media, programming, size, a rich desktop environment or it can have a general appeal. The operating system will allow you to interact with your Raspberry Pi by taking your commands such as mouse clicks and command inputs which will translate these commands and execute them. It also manages your system by allocating time to each program, monitoring it and allowing access to certain programs. Some programs are restricted to privileged users only.

Windows 10, Raspbian and Pidora are examples of a generalised operating system with various programs that allow you to configure the operating system. KODI is an example of an entertainment purpose operating system which is designed to play music, display photos and stream movies.

First time Raspberry Pi users are recommended to use NOOBS, New Out Of Box Software. This will allow you to select an operating from a menu including Raspbian, Arch Linux and more. Other operating systems that are available include Arch Linux, Retro Pie which is used to emulate older games, piCore, AROS and Debian Squeeze. There is even an Android version available although it is still under development. This is by no means a full list but it will give you a good grounding of what options are available.

NOOBS (New Out Of Box Software) is a great piece of software that takes most of the hard work out of installing and configuring the Raspberry Pi. This will allow you to select other operating systems including Raspbian. This is great if you wish to test multiple operating systems. Other operating systems exist which can also be downloaded and installed include Arch Linux, Debian Squeeze, AROS, piCore and Retro Pie which is used to emulate older games.

Before you start, make sure you have the following.

- A PC with access to the internet.
- A PC that has a card reader.
- A Micro SD adapter.

The following steps are required to get things workings.

- Download the NOOBS software.
- Extract the NOOBS software.

- Download SD Formatter.
- Format the micro SD card.
- Copy the extracted NOOBS software to the SD card.

The first thing you need to do is download the NOOBS software using a Windows, Mac or Linux computer from the address below. It is also recommended that you obtain a micro SD card with the minimum storage of 4G. The Raspberry Pi element 14 instructions recommend a minimum of 4G. They also recommend that the micro SD card should be a class 4 but class 10 also works. For this installation we used a SanDisk 16GB micro SD card that is a class 10 which can be purchased via Amazon.

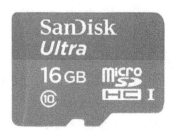

Visit the following web page on a Windows, Mac or Linux

computer.

http://www.raspberrypi.org/downloads/

Installing NOOBS Offline and Network Install

Download the ZIP or torrent file. We will only
concentrate on the ZIP file. Select the NOOBS Offline
Network Install version.

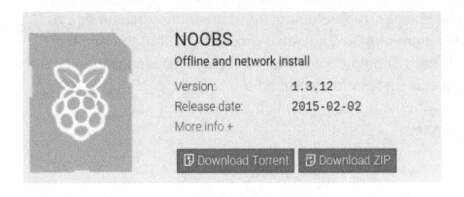

The current version is 1.3.12, release date 2015-02-02.
The difference between the offline version and the
network version is that the NOOBS LITE network version
is smaller and it will download the files required as it is
installing. The offline version will download everything
that it required including any large packages (also known
as software) in one zip file.

When the zip file has downloaded extract the contents. These files will be used later to boot the Raspberry Pi.

Download SDFormatter

For windows users

https://www.sdcard.org/downloads/formatter_4/eula_windows/

SD Formatter is compatible with

- Windows 8
- Windows 7
- Windows Vista
- Windows XP

For Mac users go to

https://www.sdcard.org/downloads/formatter_4/eula_mac

SD Formatter is compatible with

- Mac OS X(v10.8 Mountain Lion)
- Mac OS X(v10.7 Lion)

- Mac OS X(v10.6 Snow Leopard)
- Mac OS X(v10.5 Leopard for Intel Mac)

Install SD Card Formatter onto your computer and follow the instructions.

1. Insert the micro SD card into the SD card adapter and insert it into your PC.

SanDisk microSD to SD Memory Card Adapter (MICROSD-ADAPTER)

Also make sure that your card is at least 4GB.

2. Run SD Formatter and select OPTIONS. From the FORMAT SIZE ADJUSTMENT drop down menu select the ON option. Click OK.

MAC users will need to select the OVERWRITE FORMAT option from the FORMAT TYPE drop down menu.

3. Confirm that you are writing to the SD card by checking the drive letter. You can check the drive letter by making sure that the SD card you have inserted are the same. You can do this by clicking on Computer within Windows and check the drive letter.

4. Click on FORMAT.

5. Click OK to the following dialog messages.

6. When the formatting has finished it will display a message informing you that it has completed. Exit SD Formatter and copy the extracted NOOBS files that you extracted earlier to the newly formatted SD Card.

7. Eject the card safely.

Your micro SD card now contains everything you need to get started. In the next chapter you will connect the

Raspberry Pi together and explore the operating system.

Summary

This chapter took you though downloading the necessary software needed to format the SD card and copy the NOOBS files to the card. This is essential if you want to use the operating systems available. We also touched upon the various operating systems that are available and their different uses.

CHAPTER 4
SETTING UP THE RASPBERRY PI 2

This chapter will guide you through setting up the Raspberry Pi and will demonstrate the various ways in which you can connect the Raspberry Pi to the internet. The following hardware & peripherals are required to connect the Raspberry Pi 2 together.

1x The power supply. A micro USB power supply that can supply at least 600mA at 5V. Many Samsung or Google Nexus phones use this type of power supply.

1x The micro SD card with the NOOBS software that you have just written to the card.

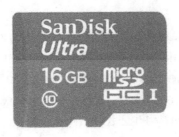

1x USB wired or Bluetooth keyboard. Wired is recommend until everything is set up correctly.

1x USB wired or Bluetooth mouse.

1x HDMI cable.

1x Network cable or a Wi-Fi nano USB adapter so that you can access the internet.

1x Wi-Fi nano USB adapter is essential if you want to connect the Raspberry Pi to a wireless network. The Wi-Fi dongle that will be used in this example is the **Edimax EW-7811Un** 150mps wireless 802.11 b/g/n nano USB adapter. This device is very fast and has a data rate of up to 150Mbps. It also supports 64/128bit WEP, WPA and WPA2 which makes it compatible with some older wireless routers and all modern wireless routers. This device can be purchased from major online stores.

Plug in the micro SD card that you created earlier into the SD card slot located on the bottom of the Raspberry Pi.

Plug in the keyboard and the mouse into the available USB ports and the Wi-Fi adapter if you are using a wireless connection.

Plug in the Ethernet cable if you are using a wired connection.

Plug in the HDMI cable and plug the other end into a monitor/TV.

Plug in the power adapter to the Raspberry Pi but do not turn it on at the mains just yet.

The completed Raspberry Pi set up should look like the image below.

Power on the Raspberry Pi.

NOTE: The Raspberry Pi does not have an on/off switch and the only means of turning it off is to kill the power at the mains.

Summary

You now know what components are needed in order to use the Raspberry Pi and you are aware of how to set it up. We discussed the various options are for getting the Raspberry Pi on the internet which included a wired network option or by using a Wi-Fi adapter. The Raspberry Pi uses a micro USB power supply that requires at least 600mA at 5V to power it.

CHAPTER 5
USING THE RASPBERRY PI

The Raspberry Pi will start it's boot up process and a message will be displayed informing you that the partition is being resized. After a few seconds the NOOBS install menu will appear. You have a number of options to select from but for now select the Raspbian [RECOMMENDED] installation and click install.

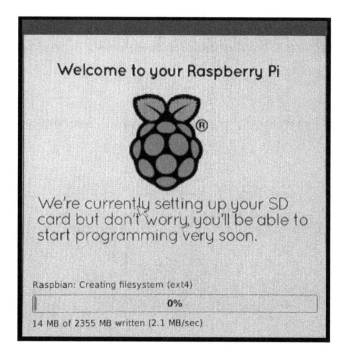

The data partition option allows an extra 512MB partition to be added to the cards partition layout and the other option will boot directly into Scratch. Scratch is a programming learning tool that has been designed to help children understand the basics of programming.

You will be presented with a warning message explaining that the SD card will be overwritten. This is OK as this is what needs to be done to install the operating system.

A progress screen is displayed to indicate the installation progress and some additional information will be displayed regarding its use. If you are new to Linux I suggest you read these tips.

You will see the following message when the installation is complete.

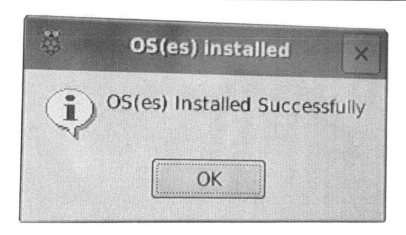

The Raspberry Pi will reboot and you will see a lot of text scrolling by. Don't worry this is normal.

When the Raspberry Pi has finished booting the Raspi-config menu is displayed. There are a number of options that you can select from to configure the Raspberry Pi. You can use the up and down arrows on your keyboard to highlight an option and press enter to select. You can also use the TAB key to jump between SELECT and BACK/FINISH options displayed at the bottom of the menu.

Expand File System

As we are using NOOBS we do not need to do this but this option allows the Raspberry Pi to use the entire space on the micro SD card. This means you may have a considerable amount of free space available on the SD card especially if you have a larger card.

Change User Password

This option will allow you to change your password. By default the user for Raspbian is *pi* and the password is *raspberry*.

Enable Boot to Desktop/Scratch

The boot behaviour enables you to select between booting the Raspberry Pi directly to a desktop, Scratch or to a command line. Modify this setting to boot directly to the desktop as later in this chapter you will explore the desktop environment. Use your down arrow key, highlight *Enable Boot to Desktop/Scratch* and press enter.

Select *Desktop Log in as user 'pi' at the graphical desktop.*

Internationalisation Options

This option will allow you to modify your language and regional settings, set your time zone and change the keyboard layout.

Enable Camera

Enable/Disable the camera if you have one.

Add to Rastrack

Rastrack is an online map of Raspberry Pi devices around the world. You can add a nickname and your email address here if you want to add it to the list of global Raspberry Pi's. The web site will map the locations of every registered Raspberry Pi.

Overclock

You can speed up your Raspberry Pi 2 by over clocking it.
Over clocking is a method of pushing the Raspberry Pi
beyond its limits. You can select from various configurations
including Pi 2 option giving your Pi 1GHz of processing
speed. Read the warning signs as over clocking can make
your system unstable. If this happens you can always hold
down the shift key while booting to disable over clocking.

Advanced options

The advanced options allow you to configure your Raspberry
Pi even further. One option included is *overscan.* As the
Raspberry Pi has been designed to work with TV's you may
find the output display only appears in the centre of the
screen and a large border. Select overscan to use this area
and select *Enable.* You will also find the memory split option.

Memory Split

This options allows you to distribute the memory usage
between the two processors that the Raspberry Pi has. The
CPU (Central Processing Unit) and the GPU (Graphics
Processing Unit). The GPU deals with graphical tasks while

the CPU handles the complex calculations. If your primary focus is games or intense graphic applications then you should allocate more memory to the GPU but in most cases a 50/50 split is acceptable.

SSH

SSH enables you to connect to your Raspberry Pi from another computer or even another Raspberry Pi. You can use a Linux terminal or PuTTY for windows to connect securely.

Update

Update is used to keep the raspi-config tools up to date. In order to run this tool at any time enter *sudo raspi-config* from a command line.

Select *Finish* when you are satisfied with your selection and your Raspberry Pi will reboot.

The Desktop

If you are new to the Raspberry Pi and Linux then it is best if you start out your experience in the desktop environment rather than starting with the command although we will visit the command line later. The desktop has been designed to make your interaction with the Raspberry Pi simple and easy. The desktop was needed to bridge the gap for non-technical users and speed up production.

There are a number of desktops or window managers to choose from when using the Raspberry Pi. LXDE, Gnome and KDE are common desktops but we will focus on LXDE because this is the default Raspbian windows manager.

Raspbian offers a fast light weight desktop that can be customised for your own desktop preferences. It has a very low memory footprint making it an ideal candidate for the Raspberry Pi. The desktop experience offers the benefits of quick menus, windows, icons, a file manager and a taskbar making some user actions far quicker than a command line.

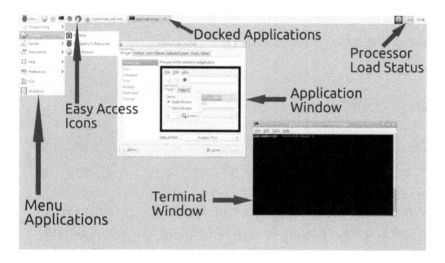

Before continuing it would be a good idea to go over some of the desktop features.

The menu

The menu organises programs and provides a convenient way to group common programs. It is where you locate most of the programs that you install.

Menu Applications

If you are familiar with the Windows or Mac OSX operating system then this will be a familiar feature. The application menu provides a fast and convenient way of grouping and accessing the installed applications.

Desktop icons

You will already be familiar with icons when using tablets and phones. Icons provide quick access to the most commonly used programs. If you want to add an icon to your desktop simply go to the Raspberry Pi menu, locate the program you wish to add to the desktop and right click on the icon. Select Add to desktop and the icon will appear on your desktop.

Application Windows

The application window focuses the users attention on the program by containing most of its central functions in one location. A window consists of a frame with a title bar, normally a way of exiting the window and common buttons to manage the window. These include a minimise and maximise button.

The Task Bar/LX Panel

The task bar or LX Panel is located across the top of the desktop. This provides a user friendly desktop panel which manages open programs and allows access to the application menu. It can be configured to your personal preferences using preferences.

Now that you understand some of the features of the desktop lets understand where the file manager fits in with this as you will be using this a lot.

File manager

A file manager will manage files and allows the user an easy interface to manage files. It provides the ability to display, copy, delete, edit, and navigate through the operating systems file system.

How to navigate

Double click on the file manager located on the taskbar. The file manager icon looks like a filing cabinet. This will open a file containing the icons that appear on your desktop. Notice that the file location now reads */home/pi*. This is your current location within the file system. This a quick reference to display to the user their current location when navigating the file system. You can use the navigate buttons to go back to the previous folder by clicking on the left arrow.

File & Folders

If you click the right mouse button, a menu will appear that allows you to create a new folder. Click on the Create New Folder option. Enter MyPi and press enter. A new folder now appears with the name of MyPi.

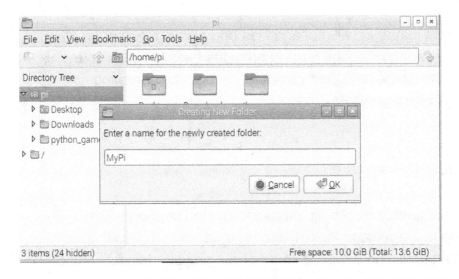

Copying Files

To copy a file right click the mouse button on a file and select copy from the menu. Navigate to the location where you want to paste the file and right click on the white area. A window will appear. Select *paste* from the menu. The file that you copied will appear in the window. You can also highlight a file and hold down CTRL and press C to copy the file and hold down CTRL and press V to paste it.

Moving Files

Moving files is a matter of holding down your mouse button on the file and dragging the file to the new location.

Deleting Files

Right click on the file you want to delete and select *Move to Trash* from the menu. A dialog box will appear prompting you to confirm. Select *Yes*. You can also highlight the file and press delete on the keyboard.

Home Folder

The home folder location located in the Go menu of the file manager contains files that you wish to keep personal. This means that other users that log in to your Raspberry Pi using a different account will not be able to access these files. It is also a good location to keep any project files that you are working on. To quickly return to the *Home Folder* simply select the *Go* menu from the file manager and select *Home Folder*. You can also hold down the ALT key and press the HOME key.

Creating Bookmarks

Bookmarks are used to quickly store and find your way to a location the file system. Navigate your way to the location and select Bookmarks from the file manager. Click on the Add to Bookmarks icon. Enter a name for the bookmark or select the default folder name. To jump directly to the location that you have bookmarked go to the Bookmarks folder and you will see the newly created bookmark that you created earlier. Click on this and the location will appear.

Connecting to the Internet

If you are using an Ethernet cable and are connected to your local network then the chances are that you can already access the internet. However if you are using a wireless adapter then you will to take some additional steps to get it connected.

Go to the Raspberry Pi menu, navigate to the *Preferences* menu and click on Wi-Fi Configuration. A dialog box will appear with a number of options. Select the *Scan* button to scan for all available wireless networks.

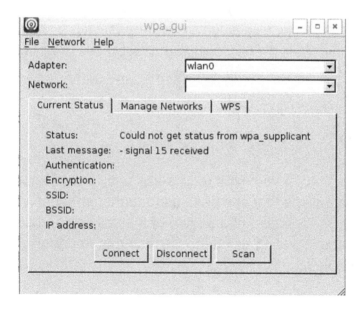

Locate your wireless network SSID and double click on the name. Another dialog box will appear asking you to enter your wireless network password. Enter the password and click on OK. After a few seconds you should see that the status has changed to connected and the Wi-Fi icon has moved to the taskbar. It will also inform you or your IP address that has been allocated to your Raspberry Pi.

Shutdown

Now it's time to learn how to shutdown the Raspberry Pi. Click on the Raspberry Pi menu located at the top left of the desktop and select the shutdown button located at the bottom of the menu. A dialog box will appear with a choice of three options. Select *Shutdown* and click on *OK*. You can also reboot or log out of this session.

Summary

During this chapter you explored Raspi-config and learned of the various options that can be used to further enhance your Raspberry Pi. You also had a taste of the desktop and some of its features including using the file manager to perform day to day activities.

CHAPTER 6
THE COMMAND LINE INTERFACE (CLI)

The terminal is a program that allows you to interact with the shell. What is the shell? The shell is a program that accepts commands from the user and passes them to the operating system for processing. Many shells exist including bash, sh, ksh, zsh and many more that offer different features. Terminals, shell and command line are used interchangeably but you just need to know that no matter which term is used, it is your doorway to issue commands to the operating system. The question arises, why do we need such an old method of accessing the operating system? In some circumstances you may not be able to access a desktop and your only access to the operating system is through a terminal via a failsafe method.

Go to the Raspberry Pi menu and navigate to the *Accessories* menu and click on the Terminal icon.

A black screen will appear with a $ prompt. The $ prompt is an indication that you can now interact with the operating system. The $ prompt at the start of the command line indicates that you are a regular user and not a super user also known as a root user. A super user has full control over the system and can issue commands that in the wrong hands can be very destructive. If you see a # prompt at the start of the command line then this is a good indication you are root or super user.

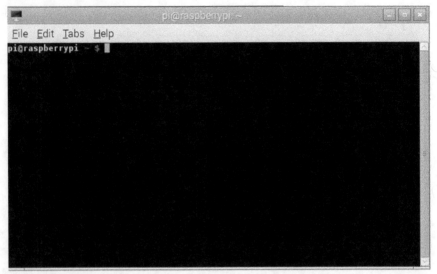

Enter the following command without the $ sign.

$ ls

The output will display a list of files because the *ls* command is understood by the operating system. Just ignore the output on the screen for now as this will be explained later.

Now enter the following and press enter.

$ iamhappy

The output is: command not found

This is correct because the command iamhappy does not exist. The shell is unable to locate this program and returns that it can't be found.

The next thing you should learn is simple navigation. When using the file system you will need to move to different directories but we must first know where we are. Enter the following and hit enter.

$ pwd

This command represents your current working directory. The output is.

/home/pi

Now that you know where you are in the file system structure, lets create a directory and move into it. Create a directory by entering the following.

$ mkdir raspberry

Nothing will be displayed as the shell only sends messages to the display when it is needed. To confirm that the directory has been created issue the ls command.

$ ls

You will see that the raspberry directory is being displayed.

Move into the directory by using the following command.

$ cd raspberry

The cd command is used to change directory but to confirm this enter the following.

$ pwd

/home/pi/raspberry

Issue the cd command again but this time we will use something a little different to take us out of this folder.

$ cd..

The .. is using the relative path meaning it will use the command based on its current location. This is helpful as you can use this in any folder and expect the same results. In contrast to this is something called *absolute path names*. The absolute path name means that you have to enter the complete directory structure. For example, issue the following.

$ cd /home/pi/raspberry

You can confirm where you are by using the pwd command.

To get back to the pi directory enter the following.

$ cd /home/pi

You can see the cd.. is far quicker than remembering and typing absolute paths. You are also able to issue system commands that perform actions outside your own workspace. For example the next command will restart the Raspberry Pi.

Remember that Linux is a multi user operating system so it is possible to have multiple people logged in from many locations. The following command will affect all users logged in.

$ sudo reboot

The sudo command is needed so that you can run the reboot command as an administrator or super user. System commands can only be executed by a super user or root user and not a regular user.

After a few minutes the Raspberry Pi will reboot. The command line prompt isn't very inviting but is extremely powerful. Other shutdown options can also be issued.

$ sudo shutdown halt

This will halt the operating system after it has shut down.

$ sudo shutdown -r 1

This command will also reboot the Raspberry Pi by performing the same command as the reboot command but will reboot after a 1 minute delay.

Shutdown is the command and -r is a flag which is used by the shutdown command. In this case the -r means reboot. 1 is the number of minutes before the shutdown occurs.

The advantage of using the desktop is clear to see because you do not have to remember any of the commands. The disadvantage of this is that some Unix/Linux servers do not have a desktop environment so you will need to learn these types of commands.

We touched upon the sudo command but some more information is required. Sudo is a command that will allow a regular user to perform administrative commands. This type of user is known as root or admin. The reason sudo is used is because it is a safeguard that prevents users from causing problems to the system. For example you wouldn't want to accidentally remove all the files from the operating system and to have the system rendered useless. Sudo will prevent unauthorised users from performing these commands.

You have examined the ls command but in order to utilise the power of these commands you really need to take a look at flags and how they can be used. Flags are used in the form of – followed by a letter. This extends the capability of the command.

Enter the following command.

$ ls

This will list any files in the current directory. This command can be extended by using flags. A flag is an additional option to the command which allows it to perform additional functions. For example enter the following.

$ ls -F

/Desktop   /Downloads   /Music   MyTextFile.txt MyProgram.py

Your output will be different depending on the files that exist in your folders.

The forward slash at the beginning of the file indicates that this is a directory. Desktop, Downloads & Music are all folders but MyTextFile.txt and MyProgram.py are files.

Enter the following command.

$ ls -l

This flag will list the files in a longer format which include the permissions for the files, who owns the file and the date that it was created. Permissions are indicated by the characters.

drwxr-xr-x

Permissions will be explained later along with file ownership. You can also combine flags to give you additional results.

Enter the following.

$ ls -lF

This will list the files in long format and will also display forward slashes / to indicate directory.

You can use the following flags to display more information.

-d list the name of the current directory
-F show directories with a trailing '/'
-a List the hidden files.
-g show group ownership of file in long listing
-l Displays details in a long format about files and directories.

-t Sort by time modified.

-R Displays all subdirectories.

-i print the inode number of each file

To expand on what you have already learned enter the following command.

$ clear

This command will clear the terminal window and the date command will display the current date. Enter the command.

$ date

Enter the following command to display some information about the system.

$ uname -a

Another great little feature of the terminal is its history. By pressing the up arrow key, it will allow you to browse the commands that you have previously entered.

File Structure

For any operating system to function efficiently and to be easily maintained by an administrator there must to be a file structure in place by which the operating system and programs abide by. For example when installing programs it is helpful that the programs are located in the same directory and configuration files are located in a configuration directory.

The Raspberry Pi core file structure looks like this. Some version may differ slightly depending on your distribution.

/
This is the top or root of the file system. You can think of this structure as a tree that is upside down. The root is the trunk and the other folders can be thought of as branches.

/boot
The boot directory contains information related to the booting process.

/dev
The dev directory contains device information including hard drives, serial ports etc.

/sys
The sys directory contains special files required by the

operating systems.

/proc
The proc directory is a virtual directory containing a list of running programs known as processes.

/etc
Configuration files and located here along with user logins and encrypted passwords.

/home
The home directory contains user data. When a user is created the operating system will create a home folder here which will have the same name as the user that has just been created. For example, if a user has been created called bob then under the home directory will be a directory labelled bob.

/root
This is the home directory for the root user also known as super user.

/var
This folder is used for files that change their size such as system and log files.

/tmp

This is the temporary directory.

/sbin

Executable files that are used for system maintenance are in this directory .

/bin

Executable files exist here that are related to operating system files.

/usr

This contains programs that are used for user installed programs.

/usr/local

This contains files that have been installed locally.

Editing Files

A common task is to edit configuration files from the shell and most Linux distributions have Vi, Emacs or Nano installed. These are common text editors that you will need to learn in order to edit files.

Nano is a text editor that is invoked from a terminal window.

Enter the following and press enter.

$ sudo nano raspberry.txt

This will start Nano with a file name called raspberry.*txt*. The menu system for Nano looks a little complex to start with but you will get the hang of it. The symbol that is represented by the ^ symbol are menu options. For example the *^X Exit* means to exit. The commands can be invoked by holding down the control key (CTRL) and pressing the letter relating to the command. The *^X* in this instance means to hold down the control key and press the *X*. This will cause the Nano text editor to exit.

Press CTRL^X to exit.

Start nano again but this time enter

$ sudo nano pi.txt

Enter a sentence into the editor and hold down the CTRL and press *X*. A message will appear explaining that you are exiting Nano and that you should save any changes.

Press 'y' to save the file.

The second message asks you if you want to save the file name as pi.*txt*. Press enter to save the file.

To confirm that you have created a file, enter the following into the terminal.

$ cat pi.txt

You should see the sentence that you entered appear in the terminal window.

Now enter

$ sudo nano pi.txt

This will load the pi.txt file into nano. From here you can continue editing the file if you wish.

There are many editors to choose from when using Raspbian and nano is very flexible and a great editor learn.

File Manipulation

It is also a good idea for you to get an understanding of how to manage files from the command line. The following topics will take you though creating, copying and removing the files.

Create an empty file called hello.txt by using the following command.

$ touch hello.txt

Confirm that the file has been created successfully by listing the files.

$ ls

To create a copy of this file, enter the following.

$ cp hello.txt hellocopy.txt

cp is the command and hello.txt is the source file or the file you want to copy. Following this is the destination file, hellocopy.txt. List the files to confirm that a copy of the file has been created.

$ ls

Remove the hellocopy.txt file by entering the following delete command.

$ rm hellocopy.txt

List the files again to confirm that the file has been removed.

$ ls

The terminal will blindly carry out your commands without asking you to confirm the file to delete. If you want to be prompted when you delete a file enter the following.

$ rm -i hello.txt

Press N because there is an additional trick left. Enter the following but this time you will press the tab file.

$ rm -i he<PRESS TAB>

This should complete the file in the command line to read.

$ rm -i hello.txt

Press Y to delete the file.

When creating files it is always nice to keep things organised.

A directory will do just the job. Enter the following.

$ mkdir myfiles

Create a file.

$ touch suntimebox.txt

List the files and folders to confirm that they have been created.

$ ls -lF

Move the suntimebox.txt file into the myfiles directory.

$ mv suntimebox.txt myFiles

List the files and folders again and take note that the suntimebox.txt file is missing.

$ ls -lF

It is missing from the current directory because it was moved into the myFiles directory. Enter the following.

$ cd myFiles

$ ls -lF

The file should appear in the directory that was created. Enter the following.

$ cd ..

Enter the pwd command to confirm your locations.

$ pwd

Confirm that you are in the /home/pi directory and enter the following.

$ rm myFiles

The output displays that you cannot remove 'myFiles' because it is a directory. This is because a flag is needed. Enter the following command.

$ rm myFiles -r

This will attempt to remove any files inside the myFiles directory before removing it.

Create another file called tempo.txt

$ touch tempo.txt

Now we will rename the file using the mv command.

$ mv tempo.txt music.txt

List the files to confirm that tempo.txt has been renamed. The mv command is used to move files but has the ability to rename the file while moving.

Summary

The terminal was explained and why it is needed and why it has advantages over the desktop. You learned the various system commands and what they can be used for. You also have an understanding of the Raspbian file structure and why each directory is used to store certain system files. Finally you learned some additional file manipulation techniques for copy, deleting and renaming files.

CHAPTER 7
WI-FI AND NETWORKING

You are on your way to finding your way around the Raspberry Pi. Although you do not need to know the technical details of IP address and wireless configuration settings, it is always a good idea to have some knowledge of how it works. You need an IP address to gain access to your network so that any information destined for your Raspberry Pi actually gets there. This is much like a house address. If someone is sending you a letter then they would need to know your address for you to receive it.

IP addresses take the form of something like this

192.168.0.1

Each device that has access to a network requires a unique IP address otherwise if two addresses are the same, the information will not know which device to deliver the information to. Most networks and out of the box routers automatically supply your Raspberry Pi with an IP address which saves you a lot of the work when setting it up. If you haven't done so already, connect your Raspberry Pi to the internet by either plugging in a network Ethernet cable into your Pi and plug the other end into your router. You will automatically obtain an IP address from your router and you can happily surf the internet, assuming it is configured to do so. The following examples will assume that your Raspberry Pi has a wired connection.

To confirm that you have an internet connection following these instructions.

Open the LXTerminal window and enter

$ *ping 158.43.128.1 -c 5*

And press *enter.*

The ping command is used to determine if a device is connected to a network and is answering requests. It is similar to knocking on a person's door and asking if they are in.

If we get a positive response from the ping command it will ask a device on the internet for a reply which will look like this below.

PING 158.43.128.1 (158.43.128.1) 56(84) bytes of data.
64 bytes from 158.43.128.1: icmp_req=1 ttl=64 time=0.342 ms

64 bytes from 158.43.128.1: icmp_req=2 ttl=64 time=0.349 ms
64 bytes from 158.43.128.1: icmp_req=3 ttl=64 time=0.381 ms
64 bytes from 158.43.128.1: icmp_req=4 ttl=64 time=0.355 ms
64 bytes from 158.43.128.1: icmp_req=5 ttl=64 time=0.411 ms

If you receive a *Response timed out* message then it is possible your Raspberry Pi is being blocked from making a ping request outside your network, the destination device isn't online or that you have typed the IP address incorrectly. This automatic IP allocation uses DHCP which stands for **D**ynamic **H**ost **C**onfiguration **P**rotocol. A configuration file named *interfaces* handles this process for the Raspberry Pi.

Enter the following into the terminal.

$ sudo cat /etc/network/interfaces

The line that calls upon an IP address to be allocated to the Raspberry Pi is

iface eth0 inet dhcp

iface refers to interface, which is the physical Ethernet port eth0. If additional Ethernet ports existed they would appear as Eth1, Eth2 etc.

Wi-Fi Configuration

Connecting the Raspberry Pi to a Wi-Fi network is straight forward providing you have a compatible Wi-Fi adapter. Make sure your Wi-Fi adapter is plugged in and you still have the terminal window open.

Open a terminal window and enter the following.

$ sudo nano /etc/network/interfaces

Nano will load a file similar to this.

---

auto lo

iface lo inet loopback
iface eth0 inet dhcp
allow-hotplug wlan0
auto wlan0
iface wlan0 inet dhcp
wpa-ssid "YOUR_SSID"
wpa-psk "YOUR-PASSWORD"

Edit the last two lines with your SSID and your wireless network password. Your SSID is the network ID that your Wi-Fi router is broadcasting. Note that your SSID and password need to appear in between the quotes.

Save the file by pressing CTRL-X followed by Y to overwrite the file. To be sure that these changes take effect reboot your password by enter the following.

$ sudo reboot

The word *auto* is used to identify the physical interface files that will be brought on or offline. The line *auto wlan0* is an example of this. It will allow wlan0 to be shut down or brought back online when using commands or when the system boots up.

The *iface* refers to the interface which is followed by eth0, eth1 or wlan0 etc ,depending on which device it is referencing. The *inet dhcp* is informing the Raspberry Pi that you require an automatic IP address in order to access the network.

If you are really struggling to get your Raspberry Pi online using a Wi-Fi connection visit this page and look for solutions that the Raspberry Pi community have found.

http://www.suntimebox.com/raspberry-pi-tutorial-course/week-3/day2-1-wireless-network-setup/

We have talked about IP address and how to configure them and we have briefly explained why you need one for the Raspberry Pi. A more in depth explanation of IP addresses are needed so you can really understand networking and the type of devices that require an IP address.

Every device from a computer to a phone requires a unique identifier to communicate with other devices on a network or the internet. If you are to address a letter in the mail then you need to address it with an exact address so that the post office know which country, post code, street address, and house number it is destined for. Most networks on the internet use something called TCP/IP protocol to communicate. This is a common standard which allows all devices to abide by rules so that each device can communicate with each other. This is no different from learning the French language so that you are able to communicate with a French speaking person.

Currently two standards for IP addresses exist and they are IPv4 and IPv6. The main different between the two is that

IPv6 is a new addition which allows more devices to be connected to the internet and at the same time be unique. With IPv4 this would not be possible because there isn't enough IP address available. Another difference is the way in which the IP addresses are represented.

IPv4 looks like this
192.168.100.100.

IPv6 is expressed like this
201c:cab7:0000:9832:0000:0000:ad01:fffa

Types of IP address?

An IP address can either be dynamic of static. You already know about dynamic IP address but we haven't mentioned static IP address. With a Dynamic IP address it can be different each time you restart your Raspberry Pi. The length of time your Raspberry Pi has this IP address is dependent on how long the router has leased this IP address for. It can lease IP addresses for days, months and even years. A static IP address however means that the IP address has to be allocated to the Raspberry Pi manually by editing a configuration file. Your Raspberry Pi will always use this IP address. This is useful if your Raspberry Pi is running a service such as SSH and you want to make sure you can always connect to it using the same IP address every time.

To change to a static IP address you first need to know your current network address, IP address and your default gateway. Your default gateway is the route that your Raspberry Pi will take to get onto the internet which will be your router.

Enter the ifconfig command again but make a note of the following information in bold. The IP address (inet addr), the broadcast address (192.168.1.255), and network mask (Mask).

$ sudo ifconfig

wlan0 Link encap:Ethernet HWaddr 80:1f:02:6c:72:7e
inet addr:192.168.1.20 Bcast:192.168.1.255
Mask:255.255.255.0 UP BROADCAST RUNNING
MULTICAST MTU:1500 Metric:1
RX packets:99 errors:0 dropped:13 overruns:0 frame:0
TX packets:48 errors:0 dropped:0 overruns:0 carrier:0
collisions:0 txqueuelen:1000
RX bytes:13047 (12.7 KiB) TX bytes:6003 (5.8 KiB)

This example will give the Wi-Fi adapter a static IP address.

Open the interfaces file and modify the following lines but using your own IP address.

$ sudo nano /etc/network/interfaces

inet addr: 192.168.1.20 [CHANGE]
Bcast: 192.168.1.255 [CHANGE]
Mask: 255.255.255.0

Your broadcast address will end in .255 (xxx.xxx.xxx.255) and the mask address in most cases will end with a zero. (xxx.xxx.xxx.0).

The following lines should remain.

allow-hotplug wlan0
iface wlan0 inet manual
wpa-roam /etc/wpa_supplicant/wpa_supplicant.conf
iface default inet dhcp

Save the file by pressing CTRL-X and select Y to save the changes.

When the Raspberry Pi reads this file when booting up it will look at the interface *wlan0* configuration and set it to a static IP address. This example has been set to the IP address of

192.168.1.20, the network to 192.168.1.0, the broadcast address to 192.168.1.255.

Reboot your Raspberry Pi with the following command

$ sudo reboot

When your Raspberry Pi reboots be sure to check the boot up information for any issues or warnings. Log back in and open a terminal. Enter the following to confirm that your static IP address is appearing.

$ sudo ifconfig

Test the connection by using the ping command. Ping your routers IP address or another computer on your network.

$ ping 192.168.1.1 -c5

This will ping response should be something similar to this.

64 bytes from 192.168.1.1: icmp_req=1 ttl=255 time=2.18
64 bytes from 192.168.1.1: icmp_req=2 ttl=255 time=2.43
64 bytes from 192.168.1.1: icmp_req=3 ttl=255 time=3.24
64 bytes from 192.168.1.1: icmp_req=4 ttl=255 time=2.20
64 bytes from 192.168.1.1: icmp_req=5 ttl=255 time=3.37

One last thing that needs to be modified is the /etc/resolv.conf file. This file contains information of DNS name resolvers that allow your raspberry pi to resolve names to IP addresses. For example if you ping www.suntimebox.com the Raspberry Pi will have to resolve this name to and IP address of www.suntimebox.com.

Enter the following command to edit the resolv.conf file.

$ sudo nano /etc/resolv.conf

Enter the following Google public dns server IP address.

nameserver 8.8.8.8
name server 8.8.4.4

Press CTRL-X to exit but remember to save the file by accepting the changes.

If you prefer you can always make a reservation on your router or server. For this you will have to make a note of the hardware address when you enter the following command.

$ sudo ifconfig

The hardware address is represented as the HWaddr:

08:00:22:ef:65:bc. Note that your hardware address will be different.

Web Browsers

Raspbian is packaged with the Epiphany web browser. Epiphany is a lightweight browser that has most of the functions available that modern browsers like Google Chrome and Firefox have. These include tabbed browsing, private windows and most recently visited web sites viewable at start up. The Epiphany icon is located on the LXPanel or task bar and resembles a world with a mouse pointer over the top.

Epiphany has improved support for HTML 5, faster scrolling, hardware accelerated video encoding and many more optimisations and improvements.

Below is a brief list of some of the web browsers that exist for the Raspberry Pi.

Midori is a web browser and like most web browsers on the Raspberry Pi Midori is lightweight and does not take up much memory. It features a search box for directly searching online, bookmarks, tabbed browsing and other features that will speed up your browsing time. The new tab icon is located on the left and is used to open multiple web pages within the browser. This is useful for quickly navigating to web pages but require existing pages to remain open. The address bar is used to directly visit a web page.

Enter the following web address.

www.debian.org

The web page will appear in the window. In the search box enter.

Linux

A list of results will be displayed related to the Linux. Click on the *back* button to go back to previous pages and forward to navigate back to the page. To search within a page hold down the *CTRL* key and press *F*. This will activate the find bar which will appear at the bottom of the screen. Enter a word or phrase to search the page. If the word or phrase is located it will be highlighted. Using bookmarks allow you to save your favourite web pages and view that anytime without remember the web address.

Click the *Add Bookmark* button.

By default the *Title* will be the title of the web site but you can change this. These details are automatically filled in by Midori. To visit a previously bookmarked web site, click the *Bookmarks* menu and a list of previous bookmarked websites will appear.

Chromium

Chromium functions much like Google Chrome and also allows you to log into your Google account. Like other web browsers this too has tabbed browsing and other features that let you rapidly bookmark and jump to web pages. This web browser supports HTML 5 video decoding which has that advantage of rendering videos. This browser places a heavier load on the Raspberry Pi but does allow for a richer experience.

To install Chromium enter the following into a terminal window and press enter. For now just blindly enter the commands as these will be explained in the following chapter.

$ sudo apt-get install chromium-browser

Press Y to confirm that you want to install the packages.

To make the browser more visually appealing enter the following.

$ sudo apt-get install ttf-mscorefonts-installer

To start Chromium go to the Menu and select Applications–>Internet–>Chromium Web Browser.

Pi Store

The app store for the Raspberry Pi is much like any other app store found with Apple, Microsoft or the Google Play store. The app store gives you access to some of the software available for the Raspberry Pi which include both free and paid apps.

To access the Pi Store login to your desktop and double click on the Pi Store icon which appears on the desktop or you can visit http://store.raspberrypi.com.

Before you can access the store you will need to register.

Click on the *login* link located at the top right corner of the window and click *register*.

Fill in your email address, password and the security question. Click on the sign me up button and you will be signed into your account. You can change your username by clicking on the edit link which allows you to change your username and upload an avatar for the account. When you have completed the above process you will see the Pi Store. A list of apps will be displayed which can filtered by clicking on the games, apps, tutorials, dev tools & media menu buttons. Next to the menu buttons appears a number. This number indicates how many apps are available for this type of application. You can also filter by tags by clicking on one of the subjects that appear on the left hand side of the window.

Note

Tags are very much like keywords so that the app can easily be searched and recognised when looking for them.

To install an app on your Raspberry Pi, click on the *Free Download* button or the *Buy* button. When the app has successfully been downloaded and installed it will appear in the M*y Library.* The *my library* button will display any apps that you have downloaded and installed previously.

Summary

You have covered a lot of ground in the chapter and should now understand why a unique IP address is needed. You also know the difference of IPv4 and IPv6 and you are fully aware on how to set up a wireless internet connection. You also know that the ping tool can be used to verify that you can contact external devices. Finally you took a look at Epiphany, the default web browser and examined the Chromium web browser before moving on to examine the Pi Store.

CHAPTER 8
SYSTEM MAINTENANCE

Adding software to your Raspberry Pi can be achieved using the apt tool or **A**dvanced **P**ackaging **T**ool. This is great tool because it provides a quick and easy way to add, remove and update programs. By default Raspbian already has wget installed but continue with the example so that you can see what the output is when you already have a package installed.

$ sudo apt-get install wget

wget is already the newest version.

0 upgraded, 0 newly installed, 0 to remove and 238 not upgraded.

The wget program is used to download files from the internet using the command line. It is extremely powerful and saves you the trouble of opening a web browser and downloading the file.

Confirm that wget is installed by entering

$ wget

wget: missing URL
Usage: wget [OPTION]... [URL]...

Try `wget –help' for more options.

Ignore the above message as this just means that wget is expecting a url to download a file from. You can also install multiple packages at once using the following

$ sudo apt-get install wget vsftp

Notice that wget is followed by vsftp. Both these packages will be downloaded one after the other. Just make sure you separate each package name with a space.

If you are not sure of the program that you want to install you can always use the apt-cache utility to search for a program. The apt-cache utility is specifically designed for searching the software package cache. The software package cache contains a list of existing software that is available for the Raspberry Pi.

Enter the following command.

$ sudo apt-cache search wget

Apt will return a list of matches related to wget.

The list of software packages needs to be kept up to date by comparing packages on your system with a remote database of updates, newly added packages and out of date packages. The following command is used to resynchronise the package index file.

$ sudo apt-get update

Enter the root password and the Raspberry Pi will obtain a list of package updates. These updates come from a number of sources online which are listed in the following file.

/etc/apt/sources.list

Enter the following to take a look at this file.

$ cat /etc/apt/sources.list

In this file you can see references to *ftp* and *http* locations which are used to obtain the software.

Deleting a package follows a similar process to the installation procedure. Simply enter

$ sudo apt-get remove wget

In this example the wget package is being removed but you can remove any package by entering its name.
The upgrade command can be used to keep your Raspberry Pi and its software packages up to date. During this process you will be informed of what packages it is modifying. Enter the following command to upgrade.

$ sudo apt-get upgrade

You will be presented with a list of packages that it will upgrade.

219 upgraded, 0 newly installed, 0 to remove and 1 not upgraded.

Need to get 517 MB of archives.

After this operation, 11.8 MB disk space will be freed.
Do you want to continue [Y/n]?

Enter *Y* to continue.

Depending on when the Raspberry Pi was last updated it

may take some time. If you only want to upgrade a specific package, enter the following command.

$ sudo apt-get install vsftp –only-upgrade

The –only-upgrade flag indicates that the package will be upgraded. Previously you removed a package using apt-get remove ThePackageName. This will leave the configuration files in place in case you ever need to install it again. To completely remove the packages and configuration files enter the following.

$ sudo apt-get purge wget

It's always nice to clean house and keep things tidy. The clean command is used to free up any disk space by cleaning up any left-over debris from the packages that have been installed.

Enter

$ sudo apt-get clean

Apt-get clean does not return any results. It just does its job of cleaning.

Connecting to your Raspberry Pi remotely using SSH

If you are working on a PC or Mac and you don't really want to plug in the keyboard to the Raspberry Pi each time then a better option is to use SSH. SSH is a method of connecting to the Raspberry Pi in a secure manner from a remote computer or device. Using this method will allow you to run a headless Raspberry Pi. What this means is that you do not have to have a monitor or TV connected to it in order to see what is happening.

Your remote computer will send commands to the Raspberry Pi and will display results on the remote computer. To send remote commands to the Raspberry Pi you will need a program to send these commands. Any terminal from a Linux computer or another Raspberry Pi will allow you to do this but if you are using a Windows computer then you will need another type of program. One such program is called PuTTY which acts as a secure terminal to connect to remote devices.

Download putty from
http://www.chiark.greenend.org.uk/~sgtatham/putty/download.html

Select the putty.exe at the top of the list of available

downloads. Putty does not need to install and is a standalone program.

On the Raspberry Pi start Raspi-config.

$ sudo raspi-config

Navigate your way to the Advanced options and select SSH. Select enable and press enter to confirm. Click finish to exit.

Assuming that all the computers and the Raspberry Pi are connected to the same local network, you will need to obtain the IP address of the Raspberry Pi. Enter the following.

$ ifconfig

Make a note of your IP address which can be found next to the line inet addr. Enter the IP address of the Raspberry Pi and make sure that the port number is 22. Confirm that SSH has been selected.

Click on the Open button and select yes when the next dialog box appears. After a few seconds a black terminal window will appear asking you for your login. Enter pi as the login and raspberry as the password.

Enter the following

$ uname -a

You should see a message displaying the Raspberry Pi version.

Services

A service is commonly known as a daemon and is one or more applications that run in the background and do not require the console to run. These daemons perform background task such as cleaning up temporary files, initialising the system, waiting for incoming connections or running databases. Some daemons will listen for connections from clients such as the Apache web server which will send out web page data when it receives a request connection.

When the Raspberry Pi boots up, the operating system starts these daemons with the use of a program called init. The init program uses a number of scripts to start and stop processes.

Each distribution has run levels and each run level contains a number of services each designated to perform certain tasks. For example you only require a basic installation without a desktop then there is no reason to load the run level with a desktop. A run level of 0 is used to halt the system and it is this run level that is called into action when you shut down the system. Run level 1 is used in single user mode only and a run level of 6 is used for rebooting.

[Not all run systems are the same for each distribution so be sure to read the documentation]

Services will sometimes need to be started, restarted, etc. Most services will allow you to interact with it from a console by calling upon scripts to do the work. Links to these scripts can be found in the /etc/init.d directory and the syntax looks like this.

/etc/init.d/the-command OPTION.

Commands that can be used are start, stop, reload, restart and force-reload. Later you will install the mySql server which is a database that is used to store information. When this is installed it will continue to run in the background. If the Raspberry Pi is rebooted it will start up each time the Raspberry Pi is started.

Users, Groups and Permissions

Every user on the Linux operating system has a unique ID and each user must have a unique user name. Users also have permissions and belong to groups which also have permissions. Groups make it easier to manage users by grouping them and assigning permissions to the group rather than individual users.

To find out which group you are in, open a terminal and enter

$ groups

You can be in more than one group and these groups have permission to access and perform certain actions.

Now enter the following.

$ ls -l

This will list the file permission in long format so that you can see the file and directory permissions.

drwxr-xr-x 2 pi pi 4096 Jan 12 2015 Downloads

The folder above is called Downloads with some strange

characters at the start.

drwxr-xr-x

These characters are the permissions and should be read like this.

The d character indicates that this is a directory. If it is a regular file it will display a-. The next characters are broken up into chunk of 3 blocks.

rwxr-xr-x

The first 3 characters are the user or owners permissions on this directory and determine what you can do with this directory but what is rwx?

Read – Read a file.
Write – Write to a file or directory.
e**X**ecute – An executable permission on the file.

This indicates that as the owner of this directory you can perform read, write and execute actions on this folder.

The next 3 characters indicate the group permission applied to this folder.

r-x

This means that the group can read and execute the file or in this case anything inside the folder. At this point you should be wondering which group? Great but for now keep that group in the back of your mind while I continue to the next block of 3 characters.

r-x

The final chunk of 3 characters are left for other users of the system or world.

drwxr-xr-x 2 pi pi 4096 Jan 12 2015 Downloads

To recap file permissions are used to limit access and are grouped together as follows.

Owner – The owner permission apply to the owner of the file or directory.
Group – These permissions apply to the group that has been assigned to the file or directory.
All other users – These permissions apply to all other world users.

Next is the number 2. This indicates how many links there are in this file. Next is pi. This indicates who owns the file and next to this is also the word pi. This indicates the group that the file belongs to. Only members of the pi group and privileged users are able to view files in this directory.

drwxr-xr-x 2 **pi pi** 4096 Jan 12 2015 Downloads

The 4096 indicates the size in bytes followed by the modified date.

drwxr-xr-x 2 pi pi **4096** Jan 12 2015 Downloads

And finally the directory name Downloads.

Sometimes you will need to modify these permissions. For example if you write a program and you want to run it from the command line you will need to make the program executable. Assuming we have a file called myprogram.sh we would need to enter the following.

$ sudo chmod u+x myprogram.sh

The chmod command is the operating system command that can change access permissions on files and directories. The character that follows this is the u character. The u stands for user and the + indicates that we will allow the following permission, in this case the x stands for execute. You can also revoke the execute permission by issuing the following.

$ sudo chmod u-x myprogram.sh

Other permissions can be set including read and write permission. Enter the following to remove the write permission to a file.

$ sudo chmod u-w myprogram.sh

And to add permission back enter

$ sudo chmod u+w myprogram.sh

Summary

In this chapter you examined how the Raspberry Pi is maintained and how apt-get can be used to do this. You also configured SSH so that you could use a terminal emulator called PuTTY to connect to your Raspberry Pi remotely. Finally we touched upon the setting file permissions using the chmod command.

CHAPTER 9
WEB SERVERS & DATABASES

In previous chapters we have explained what data is. Managing this data can be troublesome when you have many types of data. To store and retrieve this data, databases are used.

What is a database?

A database is a structured collection of related data that is used to store and retrieve data. A phone book for example is a database and the Google search engine is also a database, a very large database. Databases are used to hold a large number of records such as patient's health records, a list of blu-rays movies, a list of car registrations and owners. Databases make it easy to find information and can allow multiple users to retrieve multiple data simultaneously.

There are a number of databases available for the Raspberry Pi but MySql is a very common database in the open source community. The MySql database has the following features.

It is scalable.

It is designed for heavy traffic.
It supports user management and permissions.
It supports a client server architecture which means that you can log in from a remote computer to access the database.

A database contains tables that hold data and many tables can exist within the database. A database can be represented using the following symbol followed by a database name.

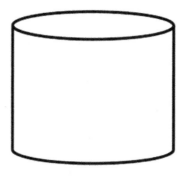

ACME ONLINE STORE

Tables

The data that is stored inside the database is stored in tables. For example when you purchase a product from an online store they will ask you for your name and address. This data might look like this.

First Name: Linden
Second Name: Roger
Address 1: 1922 Deepings Street
Address 2: Washington
Post Code: 32871
Phone: 555-5555
Email: lroger@myexampledomain123.com

The first name, second name etc. are called fields and are used to label the data that you enter.

The diagram below demonstrates how a table will look inside the database.

The data above is related to customer information. To store this related data the database will use a table called 'Customer'.

You can use any name you wish to but you should always use relevant naming. Notice that an ID field is present in the above diagram. This ID number represents the customer's unique identification number. This ID number will make it far easier to manage customer details and link their details.

More than one table can exist inside a database. For example an online store will also contain a list of products purchased by customers. The table may look like this.

Purchases Table

Customer ID: 1
Product Name: iPhone 5
Price: $200

The diagram below now contains two tables. Notice that the customer_id within the PURCHASES table relates to the CUSTOMER table ID.

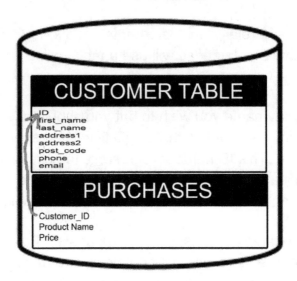

This ID provides a link between the two tables. Based on the information above you would be able to look at the purchases table and determine which customers have purchased items.

Structured Query Language (SQL)

To modify, store and retrieve data from a database you will need to use a database management system or DBMS for short. MySql, Microsoft's SQL server 2014, Oracle Database 12c and postgreSQL are examples of database management systems. Each has their own methods of modifying and retrieving the data but each uses a common language to do this. This is called SQL. SQL is short for Structured Query Language and has been designed for managing data stored in databases.

The SQL language looks like this.

select first_name from customer

The line above will retrieve all the first names within the customer table assuming the field name exists within the table.

To get started you will need to install MySql. Enter the following commands

$ sudo apt-get install mysql-server libapache2-mod-auth-mysql php5-mysql

Before pressing *Y* to continue you should examine the mySql programs that are being installed. Among these is the mysql-client 5.5 which will be used as a way to communicate with the mySql server and some additional PHP and Apache modules. These are required later when a PHP web page communicates with mySql to retrieve its data.

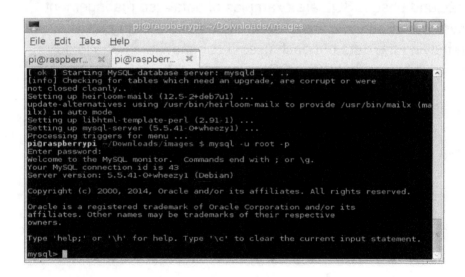

When prompted enter a password for the MySql root account. This is different to your root account for the Raspberry Pi. This password is specifically for the MySql root user. The MySql root user has special privileges so that this user can create, delete and manipulate databases.

When the installation is complete you will need to log into the mySql client shell. This will be used to communicate and issue commands to the mySql server.

At the $ prompt enter the following.

$ mysql -u root -p

This command starts the MySql client and the -u is used to indicate that the text that followings is the name of the user. In this case the user is root. The -p is used to prompt the user for a password. Enter your MySql password.

The above screen shot is the MySql monitor interface. It will be used to connect, create, delete and modify databases and tables within MySql. The interface can look a little daunting but when you have to connect to a database that is on the other side of the globe and speed is an issue, you will be glad that this basic looking yet powerful interface is available. There are alternatives to the command line and one of these is called PHPMyAdmin. PHPMyAdmin will allow you to issue commands visually using a web browser.

The next command will create a database called scores. This database will be used to store user game scores for the fictional game called Obi On The Run.

At the mysql> prompt enter the following command. Remember to complete the command by entering the ; at the end of the line.

mysql> CREATE DATABASE scores;

The database has been created but now we need to work on that database. This is done by issuing the USE command. Enter the following.

mysql> USE scores;

You will receive a confirmation that the database has changed. All future commands will be performed on the scores database. Rather than use the MySql root account to access each database, it is far more secure to create a user with less privileges. This limits any changes to this database only. The following command will do just that. The user will be called gamer and it is this user's job to maintain the scores database.

mysql> CREATE USER 'gamer'@'localhost' IDENTIFIED BY 'password';

This creates the user called 'game@localhost' with the password of password. Next you will want to setup the actions that this user can perform.

mysql> GRANT ALL PRIVILEGES ON scores.* TO 'gamer'@'localhost';

This allows all actions to be performed on the scores database for the gamer@localhost user.

The next command refreshes the database with the new privileges that you have just created and informs mySql to update its internal data with the new user privileges.

mysql> FLUSH PRIVILEGES;

If you do not issue the FLUSH PRIVILEGES command then you will not be able to login using the game user unless your reboot the Raspberry Pi. And finally enter quit to quit.

mysql> quit

You can now log in with the new user that you just created. Enter the following and enter the password when prompted.

mysql -u gamer -p

Databases use tables to store information so the next step will be to create one. A table will be created to store the scores and some additional text which will represent the player name.

Databases normally contain multiple tables which are used to store different data depending on the application. Even though this database is storing scores, it could also store a character table which could contain a number of characters to select from.

Select the database to use.

mysql> use scores;

Enter the following command to create the table.

CREATE TABLE thescores (player_name TEXT, score NUMERIC);

This will create a table called *thescores* which will contain a field called *player_name*.

This will be a text field so we will let know MySql know that this field can only store text. This is commonly referred to as a DATA TYPE because you are enforcing the type of data that can be stored in these fields. It can include numbers also such as Mike123 or just 123 but data in this field will always be treated as a text.

Finally the table will record the players score in the

field *scores*. As this type of data will be a number you can define this data type as a numeric. Only numbers can be stored in this field.

Armed with this background knowledge you can now enter data into the correct fields without receiving an error. Enter the following.

INSERT INTO thescores values('Chip Douglas', 250);

Each time you insert some data MySql will respond with an acknowledgement.

Query OK, 1 row affected (0.01 sec)

Pay attention to the name that was just entered and notice that a text string has to be enclosed within ' but a numeric number does not.

Enter the next line

INSERT INTO thescores values('Mikel Allen', 200);

Finally enter

INSERT INTO thescores values('Phil123', 400);

Now that there is some data in the table, we can retrieve this and manipulate it but first it would be nice to actually see which tables exists.

mysql> SHOW TABLES;

Only 1 table is being displayed which is exactly what we have created. To see what is in the table enter the following.

mysql> SELECT player_name, score FROM thescores;

The select command is known as a query because you are querying the database for information.

It can be a pain to type out every field name when it comes to displaying data within tables so the * symbol is the super hero in this case.

mysql> SELECT * FROM thescores;

This achieves the same result as typing every field name to display the data. You can also isolate individual columns of data by just using a single field name. For example you might only just want to know the names of the players using the game.

mysql> SELECT player_name FROM thescores;

The above command retrieves the player_name and displays them in no particular order. Adding some order to this table is just a matter of extending this query. Enter the following.

mysql > SELECT player_name, score FROM thescores ORDER BY score DESC;

You will notice that the order of the scores is being displayed with the highest numeric value first. Add the following query to display the result with a lowest scores first.

mysql > SELECT player_name, score from thescores ORDER BY score ASC;

The order clause can also be used for text fields. Enter the following.

mysql > SELECT player_name, score FROM thescores ORDER BY player_name;

You will see that the results are displayed in alphabetical [A to Z] order based on the player_name. This can also be reversed [Z-A] by using DESC for descending order.

mysql > SELECT player_name, score FROM thescores

ORDER BY player_name DESC;

You have already experienced the use of large scale databases with web sites like Amazon. Amazon store their product information in large scale databases and use a web page to query product information contained in a database. When you install WordPress later you will be doing the same thing but on a smaller scale. You will use a web browser interface that connects to a database using the PHP language to retrieve data that is stored in a database.

First you will need to install the apache web server along with PHP. PHP will be used to access the database and display the results in the browser. After installing the web server you will create a simple HTML page to verify that the web server is working and that the page is being displayed in the web browser. You may hear the acronym LAMP. LAMP is short for Linux, Apache, MySql and PHP although the P can also be substituted for Python or the Perl programming languages.

To install the apache web server, which is also known as apache2 can be installed using the following commands.

$ sudo apt-get update

The above command may take some time depending on

what needs to be updated. When it has completed enter the following.

```
$ sudo apt-get install apache2
```

Open a web browser and enter the following into the web.

http://localhost

You will be presented with a page that says **It works!**

The Apache web server is now up and running. Now you can create your own html pages. Open a terminal window and enter the following commands.

$ cd /var/www

$ sudo nano mypage.html

When nano opens, enter the following basic html code

```
<html>
<head>
        <title>This is my Raspberry Pi Page</title>
</head>
<body>This is where the action happens</body>
```

</html>

Save this file by holding down CTRL-X. Nano will prompt you to save the file.

Open a web browser and in the address bar enter

http://localhost/mypage.html

You will see a web page displaying the words "This is where the action happens". Our next step is to install PHP. Enter the following.

$ sudo apt-get install php5 libapache2-mod-php5 php5-mcrypt php5-mysql

Enter *Y* to install.

Now that we have everything required to test that PHP is working we just have to create a PHP test page. Make sure you location is /var/www and enter the following.

$ sudo test.php

And add the following PHP programming code.

```
<?php
phpinfo();
?>
```

Save the file and exit. Open a web browser if you haven't already done so and enter the following into the address bar.

http://localhost/test.php

The above screen shot confirms that PHP is working. For more information on PHP programming please visit http://php.net /manual/en/intro-whatis.php.

Summary

There was a lot of information and commands to take in during chapter. Not only did you install MySql but you also managed to create a database, a user and a table. You also managed to set user permissions so that a user can only access a specific database. You managed this with the help of the mySql client command line. You also installed the Apache 2 web server and created a basic HTML page to confirm that it was working. Finally you installed PHP and tested that this was functioning. The above chapter covered a lot but it was needed so that you can move onto the next chapter which utilises the foundations of MySql, PHP and the Apache web server.

CHAPTER 10
INSTALLING & USING WORDPRESS

WordPress can cover an entire book alone and one chapter will not do it justice but it will however give you an insight into how it functions and it's usage. WordPress is a free open source content management system or CMS for short. This means it can manage all of your web content from a browser and without the need of any programming although this option is available if you can program. Managing a web site is done by selecting a theme, uploading your images and adding your own content. You are even able to add additional users for creating content, editing or just viewing the development of a web site. WordPress started life as simple blog software but has now evolved to include shopping carts with full product stock control, numerous plug ins that extend its functionality and visual web design controls. It also has the ability to allow you to program your own plug ins using PHP but before we can see the power of WordPress, the Apache web server, PHP, and mySql we will first have to install WordPress.

The first thing we need to do is create a database that will store all the WordPress data and the content that we create. We will use the mySql client again in a terminal. Enter the following.

$ mysql -u root -p

Enter your mySql root password that was created in the previous chapter. We need to create the WordPress database so enter.

mysql> CREATE DATABASE WordPress;

And press enter.

Next we need to create a user that can interactive with the WordPress database. Enter the following.

mysql> CREATE USER wpuser@localhost;

Press enter. Next we need to create a password for this user. Enter the following.

mysql> SET PASSWORD for wpuser@localhost=PASSWORD('yourpassword');

Note that 'yourpassword' is referring to your own password which should be entered between the single quotes. Now we need to set privileges for this user so that they can access the database. Enter the following.

```
mysql> GRANT ALL PRIVILEGES ON WordPress.* TO
wpuser@localhost IDENTIFIED BY 'yourpassword';
```

This is saying that you want to grant all privileges on the WordPress database and all the tables to the wpuser. The wildcard * is used to indicate that you want to grant privileges on all tables.

Finally we need to flush the privileges by entering the following.

```
mysql> FLUSH PRIVILEGES;
```

You can now quit the mysql client.

```
$ quit
```

Now that the WordPress database, user and privileges have been setup we can now download the latest version of WordPress. Enter the following into a terminal.

```
$ cd /var/www
```

And download the latest version of WordPress by using the wget . Enter the following.

```
$ sudo wget https://WordPress.org/latest.tar.gz
```

Extract the contents.

$ sudo tar -xvf latest.tar.gz

This will extract the contents to a WordPress folder. Enter into the WordPress directory.

$ cd WordPress

Enter the following to create a copy of the wp-config.php file which we will use to edit.

$ sudo cp wp-config-sample.php wp-config.php

Open the wp-config.php for editing.

$ sudo nano wp-config.php

Locate the line that starts with

define('DB_NAME', 'database_name_here');

This line is referring to the database that we created earlier. Change the text that says 'database_name_here' to 'WordPress'.

Directly below this line is the line that contains the user name that is used to access the WordPress database. Change this to read 'wpuser' and change 'password_here' to the password that you selected earlier. This example uses 'yourpassword' in the password field. Save this file.

```php
<?php
/**
 * The base configurations of the WordPress.
 *
 * This file has the following configurations: MySQL settings, Table Prefix,
 * Secret Keys, and ABSPATH. You can find more information by visiting
 * {@link http://codex.wordpress.org/Editing_wp-config.php Editing wp-config.php}
 * Codex page. You can get the MySQL settings from your web host.
 *
 * This file is used by the wp-config.php creation script during the
 * installation. You don't have to use the web site, you can just copy this file
 * to "wp-config.php" and fill in the values.
 *
 * @package WordPress
 */

// ** MySQL settings - You can get this info from your web host ** //
/** The name of the database for WordPress */
define('DB_NAME', 'wordpress');

/** MySQL database username */
define('DB_USER', 'wpuser');

/** MySQL database password */
define('DB_PASSWORD', 'yourpassword');

/** MySQL hostname */
define('DB_HOST', 'localhost');

/** Database Charset to use in creating database tables. */
define('DB_CHARSET', 'utf8');

/** The Database Collate type. Don't change this if in doubt. */
define('DB_COLLATE', '');
```

Open the Epiphany web browser and in the address bar enter.

http://localhost/wordpress

The above screen shot indicates that WordPress is ready to install everything that is required to start creating a web site. Start by giving your web site a title, a user name , a password and enter your email address. Click on the Install WordPress button.

After a few seconds WordPress will indicate to you that your web site has been installed with the indication of a Success title.

Click on the Log in button and login using your user name and your password. You will be presented with the WordPress dashboard screen. The dashboard will allow you to create new users, create posts, pages, manage the appearance of your site and many more settings. Firstly you should take a look at the new site by moving your mouse to the top of the web page to the icon that looks like a small house. A drop down menu will appear with the title *Visit Site*. Click on this.

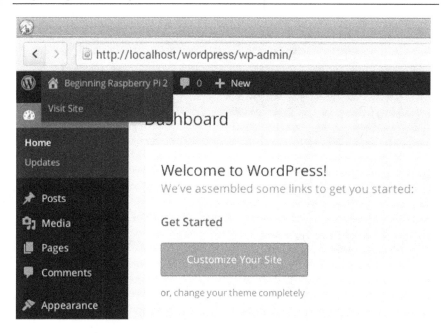

A web site will appear with the words Hello World. This is the default WordPress web page with its default theme. To brighten things up move your mouse to the top of the web page again to the icon that looks like a dial with the web page title next to it. In this case it is Beginning Raspberry Pi 2. From the drop down menu that appears click on the *Themes*.

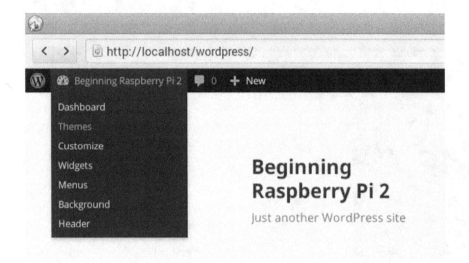

You will see three themes available from which you can select. These themes allow you to change the look of the web site. As good as these themes are I am sure there are better themes available.

A whole range of WordPress themes will appear allowing you to view their details before installing them. You can also click on the Featured, Popular, and latest themes. You can also search for a theme if you know its name. Click on the twenty thirteen theme and click on *Preview*. Click on the Save & Activate button in the top left.

Save & Activate

Move your mouse pointer to the *Pages* menu and the menu will be extended to reveal All Page and *Add New*. Click on the *Add New* button. Give the Page a Title by entering

New Raspberry Pi 2 model b

And enter the content below.

My Raspberry Pi 2 model b works well with WordPress.

Click the Publish button located on the right hand side. View the web site by moving your mouse to the House icon located at the top of the web page and clicking *Visit Site*.

The web site appears to be the same as when it was first installed. This is because we need to tell WordPress that we want the page that we have just created to be our home page. Go back to the dial icon at the top of the page but this time select Customize. Click on the Static Front Page menu and select A static page. By default WordPress will display your latest posts but in this instance we want the page to appear every time.

Click on the front page drop down menu and select the page that you have just created, *My New Raspberry Pi 2 Model B*. Click on the Save & Publish button located at the top of the page. Close this page by clicking on the X at the top left of the web page.

Your new Beginning Raspberry Pi 2 web page will appear. If you would prefer to see the web site without being logged in to WordPress just logout by moving your mouse to the top right of the web page where is says 'Howdy, admin" (or your user name) and click on *Log Out*. You will be returned to the login screen.

To view the web site simply go to the web address bar and enter.

http://localhost/wordpress/

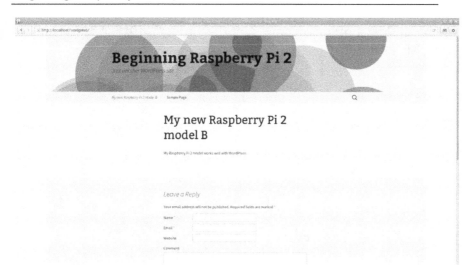

Summary

In this chapter you learned the prerequisites for installing WordPress which include a web server (Apache), a database (MySql) and a programming language that can render web pages and communicate with databases (PHP) and of course Linux. This is known as a LAMP server but other web servers, programming languages, databases and even operating systems are used to create the same result. You also learned how to install, configure and manage WordPress.

WordPress is an amazing content management program that is used in professional web design companies throughout the world so being able to install and manage WordPress is a great skill to have.

CHAPTER 11
PROGRAMMING CONCEPTS

Now it's time to turn our attention to programming for a moment so we can really start to build a picture of how computer science really fits together. Programming a computer is easier than you think. There are many computer languages available such as C, C++, Ruby and C# to name just a few. We will start off by looking at the Python programming language. Computer languages are not that different from the languages that humans speak.

The Raspberry Pi offers a range of programming languages that include Python, C, C++, Ruby, Tiny Basic, assembly and more. These languages come with a host of tools that allow you to program and examine your program code. With so many languages available which one should you select? This is normally a matter of preference or a matter of necessity. For example, PHP is a language that is commonly used as for creating dynamic web pages on the internet.

Although PHP can be used from the command line its real power is displayed on the web. If you want a fast powerful language then you would use some type of assembly language because it is faster. This does however come with a price and that price is that it is harder to understand. You will also need an understanding of the computers architecture and an in depth understanding of its hardware.

Python is a great language for the beginner because it is powerful and at the same time is very easy to understand. Python has a built in program called IDLE which is an integrated development environment (IDE). This will allow you to program directly into it and see the results line by line. This has the advantage of seeing an error before you start writing to a file.

When programming you will create a file which is called the source file and this source code is compiled or interpreted into a program. This program is executed and the results are displayed.

Programming languages have some basic common traits which include syntax, variables, control structures, data structures and the way in which they are written. A program will have an entry point which is either at the first line of the program or a specific entry point into the source code identified by a name. Each line is read and each action is performed unless the program takes a different path avoiding certain lines of code. For example consider the following.

You are at a cross roads and you can turn left or right. Your program code will execute the code for either the left road or the right but not both at the same time.

The Syntax

The syntax is the structure of statements in a computer language much like the arrangement of words that form a sentence. They must appear in the correct order so that the Raspberry Pi can understand what to do.

For example,

Stand up, turn 90 degrees to the left and walk 10 paces forward.

If this appears in this order

Turn 90 degrees to the left, walk 10 paces and stand up.

You can instantly see at the end of the sentence that the person was not standing up so how did they manage to walk 10 paces to the left.

Variables

A variable is like a box that we can store something inside and label it so that it can be opened and whatever is inside can be retrieved.

In Python this will look like this.

Number_of_penguins = 2

Number_of_penguins

We have assigned the number 2 to the Number_of_penguins. Variables can also store names.

Look at the examples below.

MyName = "Tux"
name = "Mr Smith"

A variable can store some type of value from numbers, text strings, space ships, house location, credit card numbers and ID numbers to name just a few. A variable is usually named with something meaningful that relates to the value being stored.

If we are programming a computer game and you are storing the number of lives left then a variable may look like this.

Lives = 3

This is assigning the number 3 to a variable called Lives. Another example may be that you want to store a person's name.

Name = "Homer Simpson"

Control Structures

Control decisions are used to determine which direction the program will take. For example in a role playing adventure game you may arrive at a cross roads and you have the option to turn left or right. Based on your decision the program will take a different path in the code. Here is an example.

if the direction is left then

    turn left

    walk down the mountain

else if the direction is right then

    turn right

    walk up the mountain

Another example might be to allow a player to upgrade their car if they have enough money.

If money is greater than 100

    allow the player to buy the new car

These control structures can also be combined for example,

If money is greater than 100 and the player is female then

    allow the player to walk across the bridge

Another type of control structure is a loop. A loop is a repetitive block of code that repeats and may exit when a certain event occurs. For example a person is saving to buy a computer game for $10. It's a bargain. When they have $10 or more dollars they can then make a purchase.

While the savings account is less than $9

Add $1 to the savings account

Purchase the game for $10 dollars

Each time the program iterates through this while loop, it will add $1 dollar to the savings account. The first pass through this loop contains $1 in the savings account, the seconds pass it contains $2 dollars etc. It will continue to add $1 until the savings account contains a value greater than $9.

Pseudo Code

Pseudo code is a way of describing a program and its details without having to worry about the syntax of a programming language. You have seen this already in the examples above. For example consider the following C++ code.

result = a + b;

if(result == 10) {

      //do something

}

If you not familiar with the language then this can look at bit daunting but with Pseudo code this can be explained in plain English.

Add A + B and store the answer in a variable called result.

If the result equals 10 then
    Do something

An example of a user selecting a character in game can be written using pseudo code.

Select the number of players up to a maximum 2 players

   Display characters
   Select a game character

   If player 2 is true then
       Display characters
       Select a game character

Data Structures

A data structure is a way of storing organised data making it easy to access. For example to describe a house address you will need a specific way to store this data. Take a look at the example below.

Street number = 888
Street Name = "Hill Valley Road"
City = "Edinburgh"
Post Code = "ED1 111"

Country="UK"

This data could be contained in a data structure labelled *House address* or *Location*. This type of structure really comes into play when we use Arrays. Arrays are used to store a list of similar items just like the address above.

House Locations

[1]	[2]	[3]
Street number = 17 Street Name = "Harlow Avenue" City = "London" Post Code = "SW1" Country="UK"	Street number = 9178 Street Name = "Johnson Blvd" City = "Jacksonville" Post Code = "32258" Country="USA"	Street number = 7 Street Name = "Paper Lane" City = "Paris" Post Code = "21318" Country="FR"

You can see how the data structure is common across the house locations and provide a way to access each house location by calling upon its number.

Data structures will appear often so if at this stage it's a little fuzzy don't worry you will understand them over time.

Debugging

Writing programs are never simple. You will at some point

have a bug. A bug is a problem with the code that isn't immediately apparent and therefore you will have to go through the section of code that is causing the problem.

Take the following example which should allow Jane to take out money from her bank account.

Cash_to_receive = 10

if Cash_to_receive is greater than 5 then

      dispense £5 from the account

Take a look at the above code to see if you can spot the problem.

Jane will only ever receive £5 if the amount is greater than 5 even though her input amount for £10. Debugging is an art form and you will learn more as your begin programming. Programming and debugging go hand in hand.

Boolean Logic

Computers like to test things using true and false. Boolean logic is very important in computer science because it matches the binary system which you have seen previously. Each bit is either a 0 or a 1, true of false.

In everyday life you experience this type of logic. For example examine the following the expression.

2 < 6

You can clearly see that 2 is less than 6. So it is TRUE that 2 is less than 6. The next statement is FALSE.

2 > 6

It is FALSE that 2 is greater than 6.

2 Penguins are less than 3 penguins

2 is less than 3

2 vans are greater than 1 van

Consider the following examples.

A) Is an apple a fruit? The answer is yes which is true.

B) Is an apple a car? The answer is no which equals false.

If we were to represent the above answers in a binary format then question A would be a 1 (true), B would be 0 (false). By using the binary system you are able to represent true and false values.

To represent a row of penguins in binary format that display a red star on their chest, we could use the following binary pattern.

0   1   1

Summary

This chapter introduced you to the basic concepts of programming by explaining some of the common features found in all programming languages. You have an understanding of why debugging is needed and you also have the knowledge of data structures and Boolean logic.

CHAPTER 12
THE PYTHON PROGRAMMING LANGUAGE

When programming in Python or any computer language, you will need to think like a problem solver and in time you will naturally think like a programmer. Programs are written to solve problems. Even a game has been written to solve problems while entertaining. As you build up your knowledge of programming you will be able to apply your programming knowledge to solve similar issues.

Each programming language has been designed for a particular purpose. There are languages designed for real time modelling and others for high speed database transactions. These types of languages can fall into two distinct groups, high level languages and low level languages. Python is an example of a high level language because it is removing you from the burden of understanding the Raspberry Pi hardware and thus taking you further away from the actual device.

High level languages are easier to write, tend to be shorter and are portable. This means that you can write a Python program on your Raspberry Pi and it will work on a Windows 10 operating system (Providing Python has been installed). They are also easier to debug and locate errors.

On the other end of the scale exists low level programming. These are more complex to program but have a speed advantage and take you closer to the hardware. By bringing you closer to the hardware you will be required to have a better understanding of how the hardware functions, how the memory layout has been designed and how variables are stored in the computer's memory. This can be an advantage or a disadvantage depending on your view.

Low level programs can only run on the same type of computer device. For example, if you write a program using a low level programming language on the Raspberry Pi, it will not work on an Apple Mac computer.

Even though programs are written in a high level language they will eventually be converted into a low level language. For this process to happen either an interpreter is used or a compiler. The interpreter reads a program line by line and runs it. A compiler will read the program that you have written, which is known as source code and translates this into something called object code and then executable program.

The executable program is the final result of your program which runs the program. You do not need to compile the program every time in order to run it but if you make any changes to your program then you will need to re-compile the program for the changes to take effect.

To start programming in Python we will use IDLE which will allow us to program a line at a time and see the result.

Start IDLE by going to the Raspberry Pi menu, Programming and select Python 3.

When the IDLE interface appears just press enter.

>>>

The arrows above are prompting you to enter commands into IDLE.

Enter the following lines below.

>>> johnsage = 18

>>> janesage = 21

Enter the following to display the value contained in johnsage.

>>> print (johnsage)

18

The print command will output the value contained within this variable.

>>> print (janesage)

21

You can also combine variables to obtain a result

>>> print(johnsage+janesage)

39

Other mathematical operations can be performed in IDLE.

Enter the following examples below.

>>> print (janesage-johnsage)

3

You can also create a new variable based on the result of performing actions on existing variables. For example

>>> combined_age = johnsage + janesage

>>> print (combined_age)

39

IDLE can also produce the results without the need to store numbers in a variable. For example enter.

>>> 2+2

4

You can also multiply by using the * symbol

>>> 2*8

16

To use division simply apply the forward slash / symbol.

>>> 8/2

4

Strings

Strings are a sequence of characters placed in memory one after the other to create a word.

Memory locations

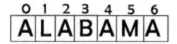

In programming this is referred to a string. Strings appear between double quotes " " and can be assigned to variables like this.

city = "Alabama"

Strings can also be added together just like numbers but with a slight difference. The string is concatenated together.

For example,

>>> "Python "+"Programming."

Python Programming.

Notice that in IDLE you do not have to use the print statement to output the result but it is good practice to use it because it will make future programming easier when you start using Python files.

>>> print("Python programming for the Raspberry Pi")

Python programming for the Raspberry Pi

When a variable stores a piece of text as in the previous example it uses a string. A string is indicated by the use of quotes " ". Anything between these quotes is a string.

A string of characters stored in memory will look like this.

0	1	2	3	4	5	6	7
M	r		S	m	i	t	h

Notice that the first character 'M' is counted as 0 and not 1. When counting each element in a string we always start at 0. A space character is also counted. The total number of characters in this string is 8.

If we wanted to get the S character you would reference this using the following Python instruction.
print(name[3])

This will print the S character.

Notice that when counting elements in a string array the starting element begins at 0.

To print the entire string you would use something like this.

print(name)

The print command is an instruction in Python that displays something on the screen. For example the following will print "Hello World".

HelloMessage = "Hello World"

print(HelloMessage)

The above program will take the string "Hello World" and assign it to the HelloMessage variable. This variable is then printed on screen.

Comments

Comments allow you to document your program as you are writing it. Comments are essential because it will help you remember why you wrote that part of the code and will also let other people that examine your program to understand it without looking at the program in detail.

To use comments in Python just enter the # (hash/pound) symbol.

#this is a comment

Notice that IDLE does not display any of the text that appears after the # symbol.

Code Blocks

Python is structured in a way that allows it to be read easily. This is done by indenting parts of the program. These parts of a program are called code blocks. Code blocks are like paragraphs in a book. They help break up the code into easy to read program code.

An example of a code block might look like this.

```
Speed = 40

if Speed = 40
    print("Slow down")
if Speed = 20
    print("Speed up")

exit
```

The arrows above are indications of indented code. This means that anything indented is contained within the 'if' section of our program and will run.

Program code can also be indented multiple times as shown in the diagram below.

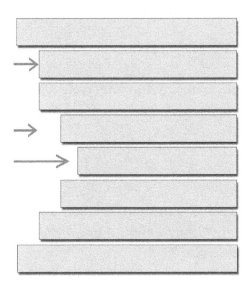

The red arrows indicate program code that has been indented.

IF

Making decisions in Python is easy. Python will use 'if' to make a decision. For example, if you want to take a driving lesson then you must be at least 17 years old. In Python it will look like this.

```
age_of_person = 18

If age_of_person > 17:
    print("You can take a driving lesson")
```

Let's add a little bit more to this python code by adding a message if the user is NOT over 17.

ELSE

Else is used when you want to perform another action based on the first 'if' statement. Can you figure out what the following message will display?

```
age_of_person = 15

If age_of_person > 17:
    print("You can take a driving lesson")
else:
    print("You are not allowed to drive")
```

The age_of_person variable is set to 15. When the 'if' statement is tested, it is found that the age of the person is 15 which is less than 17. When this happens the program will skip to the else statement at which point Python will print out that the person isn't allowed to drive.

Loops

A loop within a programming language is used to hold the program in a loop to perform repetitive actions. An example might be a delay. You might want to display a message on the screen for 5 seconds in which case you could use a loop.

In Python loops are available in many forms from a while loop, a do while loop and for loops.

While

While is used to keep your program in a loop. It works like this.

While you are playing your Xbox one
        Make sure your Xbox is online
Turn off the your Xbox

The example above is simply saying while you are playing a game on your Xbox you need to make sure it is online. This loop continues until you are finished playing the Xbox. When you are finished playing the Xbox then you will turn it off.

The Python code for the above will look like this.

```
router_is_online = true
playing_xbox_one= true


while playing_xbox_one:

    if router_is_online:


        playing_xbox_one= true

    else:

        playing_xbox_one= false


print("Turn off Xbox one")
```

The *router_is_online* variable and the playing_xbox_one variable is set to true to indicate that the router is online and that the Xbox is playing. While the playing_xbox_one is true we want to test if the router_is_online. The router is online so we set the playing_xbox_one variable to true and we return to the top of the while loop.

The 'while loop' is tested to see if the playing_xbox_one is true or false. If it is true then we stay within the while code block but if it is false the program is evaluated at the top of the while loop at which point the program immediately jumps out of the while loop and prints the word "Turn off Xbox".

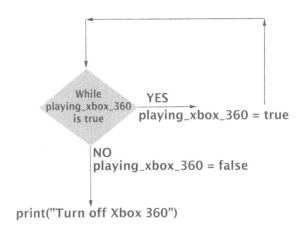

Technically you do not need to keep setting the playing_xbox_360 variable to true because it has already been set to true at the start. Take another look at the revised example.

```
router_is_online = true
playing_xbox_one = true


while playing_xbox_one:

    if router_is_online:


        #this line has been removed

    else:

        playing_xbox_one = false

print("Turn off Xbox")
```

FOR

A for loop can be used as a counter. If you wanted to exit a loop when your program is equal to 100 then you could use this type of loop.

```
for count in range(1, 100):
```

```
print(count)
```

```
print("End program")
```

The output will be something similar to this.

```
1
2
3
..

..
98
99

end program
```

You should have a basic understanding by now of how a computer program is created. In this chapter you will create a basic game based on some of the ideas previously mentioned in the chapters.

We will create a simple number guessing game. The user will be asked to guess a number between 0 and 9. The user will be able to enter a number and if the guess is correct a message will be displayed otherwise the user can continue to guess.

To start with we will create a pseudo code version.

Create a random number between 1 and 5

While the guess is not the same

      Get a number from the user
      If the number is equal
            Display a well done message

End program

Looking through the pseudo code you can see that you will need to create a random number between 1 and 5 but how will you do this? First examine the code and then we will step through the code line by line.

Create a blank file and enter the following into Nano.

```
#import the random module
import random
```

```
#create a quit variable which is used to exit when the user
has guess correctly
quit = False

#create a random number between 1 and 5
random_number = random.randint(1, 5)

#create a loop until the user guesses correctly

while not quit:

    #get a guess from the user
    guess = int(input ("Enter the guess "))



    #if the guess is equal to the random number

    if guess == random_number:


        #display a message

        print("Well done.  You guessed right")

        #set quit to True because we want to exit the loop
        quit = True

#display another message with the correctly guessed number
```

```
print("The correct number was " + random_number)
```

Save the file as *myrandom.py*.

The Raspberry Pi will use this Python source file to interpret our program and display the result. Enter the following.

```
$ python myrandom.py
```

Dissecting the code

The first line is a comment which Python will ignore. A comment is determined by the # symbol.

```
#import the random module
```

Immediately following this on the next line is an import statement.

import random

Import statements are instructions that carry out some action but do no return any information. These import statements include bits of program code that you can use. These bit of code save you significant time because you don't have to write the code yourself. The friendly Python people have done it for you. These bits of code are called modules and we bring them into our program by using the import statement.

The easiest way to think of this is to think of a large empty box, which is our program. This large box will be filled with smaller boxes that you can use later during your code. We are placing a box called random inside our larger box. The reason we are using the random module is because we need it later to generate a random number.

A variable called *quit* is created and assigned the value of False. If you were to take a look at the value inside quit after this line you would see that quit is equal to False. We use this variable to indicate to our program that we want to quit.

#create a quit variable which is used to exit when the user has guess correctly

quit = *False*

This line creates a variable called random_number which will hold a random number. The random number is generated by using the built in function random.rand() which magically appears because we use the import statement earlier at the start of the code.

#create a random number between 1 and 5
random_number = random.randint(1, 5)

The randomint() function belongs to the random module so it has to be preceded with the random modules name followed by a period of full stop.

What is a function? A function is a block of code that carries out a particular function and contains parentheses. Functions can also return a value. A function can look like this.

DisplayName()
SayHello("David")
SayHello(user)
SayGoodBye(0)
Fire(10)

The first function does not take any parameters but the next function below accepts a text string called "David". Parameters are used in functions to take advantage of code reuse, decision making, making code more generic and reduces the size of the code. As this function accepts a string, you are able to enter any name here and the function will work as normal without making any changes to the code inside the SayHello function.

If your name isn't David then you wouldn't want it displaying Hello David. You would want your own name and this is how the function works.

The next function does not contain a string but instead uses a parameter. The parameter being sent to this function is a variable called user. This has been assigned to a text string value which could be a name. The rest of the functions accept numbers which can be used to determine whom to say goodbye to and how many times to fire.

Returning back to the program code, the numbers in the randint() brackets indicate that we wish to use a number between 1 and 5. Here you can see how parameters are used in functions to determine a range of numbers for the random value. A number is returned from the function which is assigned to random_number.

Remember that random_number is just a variable that has been created to store the returned value. We could have just as easily called the variable, myNumber.

The next line in the code creates the start of a loop. A loop is needed because we will need to keep asking the user for guesses until they guess correctly.

```
#create a loop until the user guesses correctly

while not quit:
```

This piece of code boils down to this. While quit is not true, carry on reading the lines below. Notice that a colon is used to indicate that this is the start of the loop.

The next part requests that the user should enter an educated guess. Notice that this line of code is indented from the left. This is because this indicates that it is part of the loop. To indent code, press the tab button once.

```
#get a guess from the user

guess = int(input ("Enter the guess "))
```

The code above prints a message on the screen and waits for a user to enter a number by the help of the input() function. The input() function will return whatever has been entered. Notice that this function looks a little different from previous functions because it appears inside another function called int(). This will convert any string number that we enter into a real number. By default the input command has been designed to accept text string values but we require a number. So the purpose of the int() function is to convert the value to a number so that we can store it in the guess variable.

Now we want to check to see if the guess that the user has entered is equal to the random number that was generated.

#if the guess is equal to the random number

if guess == random_number:

In order to test for equality you need to use two equal signs. If they are equal then the indented code below will run. Notice again that because we are using an if statement we need to indent the code so we know which part of the code the if statement belongs to. If the guess is correct then print a message.

#display a message

print(*"Well done. You guess right"*)

Now that the user has guessed correctly we can set the quit to True.

#set quit to True because we want to exit the loop

quit = True

If the user didn't guess correctly then we do not print a well done message and we don't set quit to True. The program jumps back to the top of the loop and repeats.

#display another message with the correctly guessed number

```
print("The correct number was " + random_number)
```

Assuming that the user has guessed correctly the program will exit the loop and print a message with the random_number variables.

Python programming is fun and has endless possibilities but it does require dedication. If this is the first time you have programmed then Python is the perfect language to start with and it will introduce many of the concepts of programming that other languages have.

Many programming languages use the same ideas but express them in different ways. Just as a Chinese person will use their own language to say "I love the taste of apples" and French person may say "These apples taste amazing". They are expressing the same idea but they are using their own language to do so.

The concepts that follow are used in almost every programming language so even though the examples used will be in the Python language, the concept will remain the same across other languages.

Dictionaries

Dictionaries are used to lookup an item that you are looking for. For example you might want to look up to see if a game is available on a Playstation 4. You can use a dictionary like this.

```
games = {

    'Halo': 'Xbox One',

    'Call of Duty': 'Playstation 4',

    'Dead Space 4': 'Wii'

}
```

A key is used to access a value. In the example above we are trying to see if the game halo is available on the Xbox One. The key will be the name of the game, Halo. To find out this information you would need to use the following program.

```
print("Halo is available on the")
```

```
print(games['Halo'])
```

Functions

A function is a block of code that allows you to reuse the code at different points in your program. For example if you wanted to display your address details more than once in a program, you wouldn't want to do this every time

```
print("What is your name and address?")
print("Name: John Smith")
print("Address: 7118 Walloboro Drive")
```

```
print("Can you repeat that?")
print("Name: John Smith")
print("Address: 7118 Walloboro Drive")
```

That is a lot of typing just produce the same details. You can use a function to reduce the program code, reduce errors and make the program clearer.

Examine the following example.

```
def GetNameAndAddress():

    print('Name John Smith')

    print('Address: 7118 Walloboro Drive')


    print("What is your address?")

    GetNameAndAddress()


    print("Can you repeat that?")

    GetNameAndAddress()
```

When you want to use the function you can call it like this.

```
GetNameAndAddress()
```

The added bonus of using a function is that it will allow you to change the address in one location and no matter where you call this function in your program and it will always display the new address. Previously we would have to update the address details in two locations.

A Class

A class is a like a blue print template that holds related functions and properties which have a close relationship to the object that you are trying to create. For example if we wanted to create a dog class and everything that is related to a dog we would create a class like this.

class **Dog**:

    def **bark**():

       print(*"Woof woof"*)

    def **getName**():

       print(*"The dog is called Raspberry Pi"*)

The keyword class is used to indicate that we want to define a class called Dog. We then add the methods that are relevant to a dog. Methods are the same as functions except they are called methods when the function is contained within a class and start with the def keyword.

To actually use the Dog class and use its methods we will have to do the following.

```
dog = Dog
```

```
dog.getName()
```

```
dog.bark()
```

First we create a variable called dog and assign a variable to create a copy of the Dog class. This will now give us access to the functions in the Dog class. To call a function, use the following.

```
dog.name_of_the_function
```

The . symbol allows us to access a method of the dog class.

Summary

You explored the syntax and structure of the Python programming language and how this syntax, although strange looking at first, can be used to create powerful programs. You should understand how the import feature can be used to allow you to utilise existing program code in the Python libraries and although we only examined Python terminal programs, Python can be used to interact with external sensors with very little effort. It can also be used to create wonderful 3D computer games with the use of PyGame.

Hopefully this chapter has given you some basic information on the Python programming language and what can be done with it.